MW00860765

The Ageless Wisdom

TORKOM SARAYDARIAN

T.S.G. PUBLISHING FOUNDATION

Visions for the Twenty-First Century®

©1990 THE CREATIVE TRUST

All Rights Reserved

No part of this publication may be reproduced, stored in a retrieval system, or transmitted in any form, by any means, electronic, mechanical, photocopying, recording or otherwise, without permission in writing from the copyright owner or its representatives.

ISBN: 0-929874-13-7 (Softcover)

Library of Congress Catalog Card Number 89-51507

Cover design: *Fine Point Graphics*
                  Sedona, Arizona

Printed in the United States of America

Printed by: *Delta Lithograph, Co.*
                  Valencia, California

Published by:

T.S.G. Publishing Foundation, Inc.
Post Office Box 7068
Cave Creek, Arizona 85331-7068 U.S.A.

NOTE: The meditations and prayers contained in this book are given as guidelines. They should be used with discretion and after receiving professional advice.

Table of Contents

Whoever in speaking attributes the Teaching of Life to himself falls into falsehood. The Sources of the Teaching are beyond human limits. The Truth has been written down in Infinity, but each day it reveals a new hieroglyph of its eternalness. Mad is he who while on Earth arrogates to himself the Teaching of Life. The loftiest sage considers himself a messenger. Not the new is proclaimed, but what is needed for the hour. The steward summons to the meal; this is not new, but for the hungry it is extremely important. So much the worse if someone obstructs the call to a meal. He who hinders forges shackles for himself.

Brotherhood, para. 283

Foreword

When science grows at the expense of spiritual progress or moral development, Nature violently reacts in the form of massive destruction. This is true for individuals as well as for nations and for humanity as a whole.

The Teaching is the only means to evoke benevolent forces from Nature which will not only protect the advancement of the human spirit but will also annihilate elements destructive to human advancement.

Torkom Saraydarian
1989

Four Cosmic Truths

1. In each human being there is the Spark, the seed of the Self that transcends time and space.

2. This Self has seven main characteristics: Light, Love, Beauty, Power, Immortality, Freedom, and Infinity.

3. The Self is always in contact and in communication with the All Self, though often not conscious of It.

4. Each Self is a Ray projected from the All Existing Self—the One Source.

The Twelve-Fold Path

The Four Cosmic Truths can be actualized by the Twelve-Fold Path:

1. Right Observation

2. Right Concentration

3. Right Meditation

4. Right Contemplation

5. Right Illumination

6. Self-actualization

7. Compassion

8. Renunciation

9. Conscious Striving

10. Sacrificial Service

11. Creativity

12. Synthesis

Those who will understand the Four Cosmic Truths, actualize this Twelve-Fold Path, meditate on both will enter into the Path of Conscious Immortality.

Chapter One

The Symphony

The Ageless Wisdom, or the Teaching, is a symphony of ideas collected and related together in such a way that they reflect the highest Wisdom given by Cosmic Minds.

Through ideas, archetypes are reached in which the human soul realizes the relationship of energies and matter which sustain the manifestation of a solar system or a galaxy.

In every cycle the symphony of ideas is played in a new key to clear away the crystallizations in the human mind and then to open a new way leading to the Highest.

As human understanding develops and consciousness expands, man touches new tides, new currents of ideas, through which hidden corners of his nature come into existence.

The Teaching is the meeting point of two mighty currents of energy: experience and revelation, wisdom and knowledge.

People do not realize yet that just as a man thinks, so the planet thinks, the solar system thinks, the galaxy thinks, the Cosmic Whole thinks. Thoughts from such higher sources scattered in Space nourish the human soul and open it step by step to the labor of higher and higher creativity.

All pure thoughts form a symphony in Space. Man grows by merging his mind into the symphony of these thoughts, behind which exist the world of ideas, the world of archetypes, and the Mighty Minds. The Ageless Wisdom, the Teaching, is the network of light relating all these mighty currents of creativity.

To study the Ageless Wisdom means to fuse your soul with the mighty currents of creativity.

People sometimes think that the Teaching is contained in books written in the past six-thousand years, but much earlier records have been found. These records were found not only on certain kinds of metals but also on stones, on walls of ancient ruins, and on rocks of certain mountains. The Teaching is found everywhere upon the Earth, especially in ancient volumes, under various names, hidden in mountain caves.

There are records of Wisdom older than fifteen million years. This is a hallucinatory statement for some people, but, for those whose minds are open, the Earth has many surprises and many treasures. There are records related to the Atlantean civilization and even the Lemurian civilization. We are talking about records fifteen to twenty million years old.

Human experience and knowledge gained from higher sources always exist, but sometimes they are hidden in order not to lead unprepared people into danger.

The Teaching in its entirety exists in Space. Soon, people will be able to read the scrolls of Space on which the Wisdom of all races since the beginning of this globe has been recorded.

Man believes that all his information is drawn from books and experience, but in reality a major part of our knowledge comes from the scrolls of Space.

If humanity advances in group consciousness, new discoveries will be given to enable us to read the scrolls of Space. These scrolls surpass the contents of all the libraries in the world.

Most of the ancient records are locked behind iron doors or in caves, and they are not available to average human beings. But the libraries of Space are always open if we have the light of intuition to enter in.

The Earth, according to the Ageless Wisdom, went through four cataclysms due to subterranean convulsions and "by successive disturbances in the axial rotation of the earth." But always it was possible to save those records which contained the essence of the Teaching.

The treasury of Space and Earth contains all the Wisdom. This Wisdom is available to those who are pure in heart.

The Ageless Wisdom is not historical information but the treasury of the knowledge of self-actualization. Every page in the Ageless Wisdom urges us to be something higher than we are in our beingness, urges us to offer something greater to humanity than what was offered in the past.

Chapter Two

Ageless Wisdom

The Ageless Wisdom is not only that Wisdom which is given or revealed, but it is also the sumtotal of the experiences, knowledge, and wisdom harnessed by humanity.

The Ageless Wisdom is not a book but the collective Wisdom of humanity, the treasury of the human soul.

The Ageless Wisdom is the small part of that Wisdom which the Mighty Life of our galaxy brought to the galaxy billions of ages ago from the unfathomable source of Space and gave a portion of it to our Solar Life—or Solar Logos—and He in His turn gave a tiny part of it to the Guides of our planet, and They in Their turn gave a still tinier part to those who had the capacity to think.

The Ageless Wisdom does not belong to privileged people. Every human being can have access to it, if he wants to pay the price: a steady striving toward Light and Beauty.

Knowledge, experience, and wisdom are not gained only in our waking consciousness. There are many other planes of existence where we gain knowledge, experience, and wisdom. Though we cannot often remember them, we use them in our daily practical life.

Subjective knowledge, experience, wisdom, and revelations are given to us daily by those who broadcast them on various levels. We subjectively hear them, sometimes record them, but when we become occupied with our physical life, most of them vanish like a sweet dream.

The possibilities to gain wisdom, knowledge, and have certain experiences and revelations are not limited to our five senses on the physical plane. Some of us live on higher and higher planes, which people call astral, mental, Intuitional, and still higher planes. For some people the field of experience is not only the physical plane but also the astral, mental, and other planes where they function with subtle senses that carry information to their five senses.

We often resemble fish who have no awareness of the computers, tape recorders, or laser equipment in use today. Our entire knowledge on the present plane of existence, in comparison to the knowledge on higher planes, is just like that of a fish.

The Ageless Wisdom is the accumulated instructions given to us since the beginning of human history. It is also the accumulation of all those experiences that outstanding souls have had and have transferred to us orally, in symbols, through carvings, or in books. For example, the myths of all nations are the precious heritage of the Ageless Wisdom. Scientific and religious revelations are part of it.

Wisdom is gained not only through learning and knowing but also through experience, through becoming personally involved with the revealed laws and principles and trying to apply them in life.

It must be added that wisdom is not limited to any one field of human endeavor. There is political wisdom, wisdom in the educational field, wisdom in the field of communication, wisdom in the arts, wisdom in the scientific field, wisdom in the religious field, and even deep wisdom in the field of economy.

The Ageless Wisdom does not belong to any party, to any nation. It is the heritage of all nations.

The enemies of human progress are always ready to persecute those who bring in a new phase of the Teaching to humanity. For example, during the period of the Inquisition the students of Wisdom, or free thinkers, were called the enemies of religion and put to death. The Inquisition called such people who practiced or studied the Ageless Wisdom "sorcerers," "witches," "black magicians," "wizards," "slaves of the black arts," "enemies of religion," "enemies of humanity," "friends of Satan." One wonders how people who harm others are going to pay their debts to Nature's Law of Righteousness.

The difference between knowledge and wisdom must be clear in our mind. Knowledge is recorded information about life forms and events; formulations about laws governing our solar system and beyond; information about how life forms and chemicals affect us and how we can use them for our pleasure, greed, or satisfaction.

Wisdom is knowledge plus love. In wisdom, knowledge is used to help people strive toward their ultimate destiny, to create unity and synthesis, to reveal latent potentials in man and use them to achieve health, happiness, prosperity, success, and for enlightenment on a global level.

Wisdom is not only occupied with creating a wonderful world to live in, but it is also occupied with eradicating all causes of suffering and pain.

Wisdom is a mixture of love, knowledge, and revelation. Only wisdom can make safe the knowledge accumulated throughout ages. Only wisdom can solve problems that bring good to all men everywhere. Only wisdom can open the gates of the spiritual heritage of humanity.

Wisdom is charged with deep compassion and enlightened by the purpose of life.

The Ageless Wisdom is the knowledge, experience, and revelation accumulated throughout the ages and charged with pure compassion.

In a sense all our schools, colleges, universities, and private institutions are preparing people eventually to have wisdom.

When knowledge, experience, wisdom, revelations, and compassion are combined—we call it the Teaching. Those who can teach the Teaching are called the Great Teachers of humanity, such as Buddha, Christ, and other Great Ones.

Revelation makes a person understand the things he has learned. It makes him see objects on all planes simultaneously, where before he only had knowledge of them on one or two planes. For example, you know the color of certain notes on the physical plane. When revelation occurs, you can see the different shades of that color on all planes. You know what love is on the physical plane; when you have a revelation, you see what love is on various other planes.

What is inspiration? Inspiration is wisdom impressed on your soul from a Higher Source which seeks expression. The wiser a person is, the greater his expression of the incoming inspiration will be.

The Teaching never contradicts the true science. Actually, the Teaching uses every true revelation in science—but it does not encourage science to pollute the Mother Earth and make it difficult to live for all living forms.

The Teaching not only accepts pure science, but it also synthesizes the sciences of politics, education, communication, philosophy, religion, the arts, and economy.

The greatest characteristic of the Teaching is all-inclusiveness. That is why fanaticism and totalitarianism cannot breathe in the Teaching.

The Ageless Wisdom is the formulation of Divine Intent. When a person builds a chair, he has an intention; he will use it to sit on or he will sell it. Similarly, it is impossible to imagine that all that exists in the Universe is not created by some Divine Intent.

Why should all that is in creation exist? Why was everything created? There should be some intent. The Ageless Wisdom formulates this Divine Intent and gives us various techniques to understand Divine Intent.

The Ageless Wisdom says that all human beings have the capacity to search for and understand Divine Intent. By thus explaining the Divine Intent, the Ageless Wisdom brings meaning and direction to our lives in this confused world.

The Ageless Wisdom teaches that some great minds formulated a Plan which, if fulfilled, will result in the revelation of Divine Intent in our soul. The Ageless Wisdom not only speaks of Divine Intent, or Purpose, but also of the Plan, the Divine Blueprint.

The Plan is occupied with answering "How?". . . How can we accomplish bringing Divine Intent into our own lives, into our national and planetary lives? How can we bring about cooperation, peace, and understanding? How can we free the human soul from the prisons of attachment, vanity, and ego? How can we build the global temple, and what materials should we use? All goal-fitting answers are parts of the Ageless Wisdom.

The Ageless Wisdom is the path which leads to synthesis and unity. Every knowledge, every action, every cooperation in light, every service, every work of art which leads to synthesis, knowledge, and beauty is inspired by the Ageless Wisdom.

The purpose of the Ageless Wisdom is to create synthesis. Each part and expression of the Ageless Wisdom stands for unity and synthesis; it teaches the steps of how to reach unity and synthesis.

The Ageless Wisdom teaches goal-fitness. It emphasizes that nothing should be done to waste energy, time, matter, and space. All our actions, words, feelings, and thoughts must be in harmony with the Divine Plan and Intent.

The Ageless Wisdom encourages all human beings to think in terms of one humanity, in terms of one solar system. The Ageless Wisdom suggests that humanity consider this planet a house in a larger neighborhood, and it advises us to take special care of our house to keep the neighborhood happy and creative.

Every goal-fitting act is a practical action. Goals are stations which lead the train to its final destination.

The Ageless Wisdom is the Teaching of Beauty, Goodness, Righteousness, Joy, and Freedom. It says that all creation is the seed of a rare flower and that this seed must grow, unfold, and open its petals in Space to manifest the glory hidden within its Core.

Those minds that are "cracked" because of wrong doings and bad karma in the past can no longer use pure logic and reasoning, and in stupidity they choose ugliness combined with crime and violence. Ugliness is a sign of degeneration. In these days, because of advanced technologies, people are able to see ugliness in movies and theaters, presented and covered over with colorful and exciting "cosmetics."

We must remember that the Ageless Wisdom is the Beauty, Goodness, Righteousness, Joy, Freedom, and Wisdom found in all traditions, religions, arts, sciences, ceremonies, communications, and political ideologies. None of these are complete in themselves; none of them completely encompass or exhaust the Ageless Wisdom. Each of them is a minute piece which compliments the others, like pieces of a jigsaw puzzle which, when the pieces are placed in their right order, eventually have meaning and significance. Each portion works to complete the whole picture.

But all too often people are stuck with what they have, assuming that their little part is the whole. How can it be the whole if, from the perspective of the Cosmos, we see the minuteness of our capacity to contain Wisdom? My Teacher once told me that each branch of Wisdom is just a single hair on the Head of God. "Our intention," he said, "is not to be stuck with one hair but to find the Head and discover that, though the Head is one, It has billions of hairs."

All of the branches of knowledge, when crystallized by definitions, and when unrelated to other branches, eventually become "the only way to fly." This brings great danger to humanity because "the only way to fly" eventually misuses itself and loses its balance, proclaiming that it is the only "hair on the Head." Fanaticism and bigotry in all these forms are sources of pain and suffering, as well as being impediments and hindrances to those who are ready for a much higher Wisdom.

Any crystallized formulation of laws and principles acts against those laws and principles. Formulations, dogmas, doctrines, and catechisms are the causes of the weakening and eventual disappearance of the spirit of the laws and principles.

Great geniuses are those whose definitions are not like coffins—in which they bury a law or principle—but are like observatories through which we can better see the stars.

The enemies of religion or of any branch of knowledge are those who try to make that religion or field of knowledge absolute, infallible, superior, who try to prevent people from searching and discovering more as they grow and mature.

People often try to encapsulate their wisdom into "pills" of interest which can be consumed by their followers. Such people do not feed their followers but make them into a separate species.

No Teaching of a Great One is separative. Their Teachings build ladders to climb to the summit of the Temple. A ladder is never mistaken for the Purpose. All formulated and delivered Wisdom is a ladder which leads to the Purpose. When people lose sight of the Purpose, the ladder then becomes the object of their worship, and they are stuck, perpetually going up and down, assuming that they have already found that for which the ladder was constructed.

Chapter Three

Manifestations Of The Ageless Wisdom

The Ageless Wisdom manifests through many traditions, religions, philosophies, and Teachings. The duty of the student is to see the one essence which runs through all of these. When the essence is seen, there will be no fanaticism, imposition, or confusion.

Differences come into being because of the different levels of the minds of those to whom the Teaching is given and because of different needs in different cycles.

What are the main, or principal, Teachings of the Ageless Wisdom?

- To manifest Beauty

- To release Goodness

- To establish Righteousness

- To increase Joy

- To spread Freedom

- To encourage striving toward perfection

- To perform sacrificial service

These seven principles are the seven paths upon which the student of the Ageless Wisdom walks.

Beauty is the bridge between the archetype and its manifestation. When this bridge is built, transforming energies do their job.

Goodness is the attunement of your life with the Heart of Compassion in the Cosmos.

Righteousness is the active presence of divine accuracy and justice.

Joy is the manifestation of the free flow of your essence—when there are no hindrances on its path. It is the fragrance of the flower of purity.

Freedom is the ability to move beyond all limitation, definition, formulation, and formation. Freedom is the Holy Spark, traveling toward all inclusiveness.

We strive toward perfection through the following methods:

- Unlearning

- Renouncing

- Passing from complexity to simplicity

- Working to reach the Divine Self

Sacrificial service is a directed effort to restore the free circulation of Light, Love, and Power to all living forms by untangling the Spirit which is tied to physical traps, emotional glamors, ego, vanity, intellectual crystallizations, dogma, doctrine, and definitions.

The Fundamentals of the Ageless Wisdom

The Ageless Wisdom makes these statements:

1. In order to become a divine, fully conscious God...the Spiritual Primeval Intelligence must pass through the human stage.[1]

---

1. H.P. Blavatsky, *The Secret Doctrine,* 3rd rev. ed., 3 vols., (London: Theosophical Publishing Society, 1893), vol. I, p.132.

2. It is the ONE LIFE, eternal, invisible, yet omnipresent, without beginning or end . . . .[2]

3. Humanity and the *Stars* are bound together indissolubly, because of the *Intelligences* that rule the latter.[3]

4. Creation is but the result of Will. . . .[4]

5. [There is] an Omnipresent, Eternal, Boundless, and Immutable *PRINCIPLE* on which all speculation is impossible.[5]

6. The Absolute universality of that law of periodicity, of flex and reflex, ebb and flow.[6]

7. Fundamental identity of all souls with the Universal Oversoul.[7]

How to Approach the Teaching

The Teaching is approached through discrimination and discernment. This science cannot be developed by increasing your information or wealth, or by climbing to higher positions in society, but only through the discipline of purification on the three planes of personality: physical-etheric, astral, and mental. Purification is achieved through the following three methods applied simultaneously:

---

2. *Ibid.*, p.32.
3. *Ibid.*, vol. II, p. 368.
4. *Ibid.*, p. 183.
5. *Ibid.*, vol. I, p. 42.
6. *Ibid.*, p. 45.
7. *Ibid.*

1. Elimination of elements of pollution on the three planes

2. Meditation

3. Sacrificial service

1. Elimination of elements of pollution. What is pollution? Pollution is a condition in which cells, organs, glands, feelings, and thoughts lose the purpose of their existence and become abnormal and self-defeating. All vices are pollutants. Inertia and depression lead to pollution.

Every kind of hallucinogenic drug, marijuana, tobacco, alcohol, sexually transmitted diseases are major pollutants of the physical body. Hatred, fear, anger, jealousy, and revenge are pollutants of the emotional body. Greed, vanity, ego, separatism, and fanaticism are sources of pollution of the mental body.

Self-interest is the axis of all pollution. A person who lives in such pollution must not approach the Teaching. Instead, he must seek a Teacher who can clean his nature. Cleanliness and purity are the foundation of the Teaching. The Ageless Wisdom is extremely dangerous for those who have unclean motives and unclean hearts.

2. Meditation. Meditation helps a person digest the Ageless Wisdom and make it a living factor in his life. Here we must emphasize that if you start doing meditation, you must continue it or else you will be useless or even dangerous. Meditation makes you assimilate the Wisdom. Without digestion, your emotional and mental mechanisms will create various problems for you.

Meditation must be regular and continuous and must be done only fifteen minutes a day, at most, for the first three years.

Meditation builds a great fire in the mental plane which draws negative elements from the subconscious mind and slowly burns them, eliminating future dangers of invasion from the subconscious mind. When you stop meditation, the fire slowly dies out while the flow from the subconscious continues and fills your mind with negative elements. These negative elements devastate your life and feed your negative and destructive tendencies to such a degree that you work against your own survival and the survival of others.

When you meditate in the right way, you not only clean your subconscious mind, but you also draw treasures from your Chalice and enrich your consciousness to such a degree that you become a fountain of creativity and beauty.

3. Sacrificial service. Sacrificial service is a means through which you can draw energy from your Core—which is the Treasury of Wisdom. A student of the Ageless Wisdom never advances unless he learns how to serve and unless he finds daily opportunities to serve others in joy and without self-interest.

Discrimination is an essential part of your approach to the Teaching. In choosing reading material for example, you may wonder how you can know whether or not a book contains a fantastic Teaching without reading it. The answer is that when you have a sense of discrimination, you "smell" it before you read it. A dog smells a piece of meat to find out whether or not it is rotten and will not eat it if it is. If he ate the meat without smelling it first, he would poison himself and

it would be too late for him to find out that it was
spoiled. Similarly, by reading a "rotten" book, you have
already polluted your consciousness. A sense of discrimination saves you from reading the book.

If your sense of discrimination is not very active,
read a sentence or a paragraph and then toss the
material away if your intuition tells you not to read it
at all. You must develop the sense of discrimination or
intuition. Do you drink a cup of liquid to find out what
it is? First you smell it. Then you may dip your finger
in the cup and taste just a little. Or you may send it off
for analysis, and so on. Before you read a book, you
must know who the author is and what kind of life he
has lived, what his philosophy is, what religion he
practices, and what are his goals in life. All of this
information can tell you whether or not to read his
book.

A person once brought me a book with a fantastic
cover. I knew the author was a man who used various
drugs and encouraged others to do the same, so I said,
"I don't like to read books written by this author." The
person replied, "Well, you are a prejudiced and nar-
row-minded fanatic." I told him, "Even with such accusations, you cannot make me read that book." Years
later the person became a drug user. When he finally
saw his own destruction, he searched for help from
various organizations. Eventually, after losing his job
and his wife, he came to me and said, "You know, it
was that book which ruined my life." "You are a
fanatic," I said to him, reminding him of what he had
said to me in the past. "Well," he said, "I withdraw my
accusations; you were right." But he realized this only
after a great tragedy.

Discrimination saves your life. Try to develop the sense of discrimination by all possible means. Purify your nature, and your sense of discrimination will grow and unfold.

Beware of those who advise the use of drugs in conjunction with the Teaching and meditation.

Beware of those who think that life is a joke, a purposeless drama or comedy.

Beware of those who are "prophets," "sages," or the "incarnations of Great Ones."

Beware of those who use you for their own separative policies and who manipulate you and use your resources to climb to higher positions.

Beware of those who praise you, flatter you, or bribe you. They will lead you into an undisciplined life.

The Ageless Wisdom never encourages showing off. It encourages humility, simplicity, and inner work—inner transformation.

The assimilation of the Ageless Wisdom will manifest through an increasing joy in your life—through greater discrimination, through more sacrificial service, and through a greater hunger for Wisdom. If you meditate or think upon these factors, the traps of the dark forces will probably not catch you and you will grow and develop into a great beauty in the light of the Ageless Wisdom.

There are two ways in which you can hurt yourself:

1. By reading or studying the Teaching without being able to assimilate it.

2. By reading and "understanding" the Teaching without applying it in your life.

In the first case you waste your time and money and fall into confusion. In the second case you create conflict and cleavages within you. But if you read and see the usefulness of the Ageless Wisdom and then apply it to your life, you will become an integrated human being.

Remember, "A house divided against itself cannot stand."

How to Plan Your Studies

Before you start to study the Ageless Wisdom, draw up a plan and follow it, changing it as necessary. This plan must include

1. which books to study

2. how long to study daily

3. how to study (reading intellectually and intuitively, reflecting and making an effort to understand)

You should not read several books at once on the same subject. Finish one book, then pass on to the next. Of course, you can spend two hours reading about the Ageless Wisdom in philosophy, science, art, physics, chemistry, and economics. But whichever subject is chosen, it must be studied carefully with your entire attention until you feel that you know enough about the subject for the time being. Then go on to the next subject.

Before you choose a book, you may ask someone to help you who is an expert in that particular field.

There are very important books in the field of politics. You can find them and see if they are dedicated to the Common Good.

There are very important books in education. You can read them if you are interested in that field.

There are many important books on philosophy. Besides the classics, you can read books on Buddhism, the *Upanishads, Bhagavad Gita, Vishnu Purana, Vedas;* writings of H.P. Blavatsky, Patanjali, Shankaracharya, and Alice A. Bailey, as well as the Agni Yoga Society books.

There are many excellent books on art. You can read about Nicholas Roerich as well as books written by him and by other great artists.

There are excellent books on science in general as well as on specialized branches of science. Choose a wise teacher and ask him what books he recommends. Remember that your real training starts after you graduate from the university.

There are excellent books on religion. I would suggest the *New Testament* and the *Lotus Sutra* and books on other religions. It is wonderful to read about other religions with an open mind.

In the field of economy you will find some good classics, but try to find new books which deal with the principle of sharing and global economy.

But after you read various books related to one field, try sometimes to read books that are related to other fields. This way you expand your consciousness and do better in your own specialized field.

There are many people who are philosophers but also interested in the arts; politicians interested in economy; educators interested also in religion or politics, and so on. It is good to have an expanding mind—and also a well grounded mind. Fanaticism in any field puts a stop to your progress. Narrow minded people cannot succeed in an ever expanding world.

But through all these Teachings, develop intuition because intuition sees beyond knowledge, information, and data. And the best device to learn the Ageless Wisdom is to read the Book of Life through keen observation and intuition.

Make a yearly plan or a ten-year plan. For example, you can study X, Y, and Z over the next ten years so that you can teach Z, write about X and Y, and organize lectures and seminars about X.

If your plan is clear, you will save energy, time, and money, and you will not get lost in the confusion of visiting hundreds of different teachers and groups, or of learning from an endless number of books.

It is necessary to find a Teacher. *Challenge for Discipleship* can be an exceptional guide for you in choosing a Teacher.[8]

The Ageless Wisdom is not limited to the publications referenced above. There are other sources which you may find, but you must be careful not to be trapped and dulled by any teaching.

Consciousness and Beingness

The main goal of the Ageless Wisdom is to expand your consciousness and to elevate the nature of your beingness. Consciousness and beingness are two different states of the human soul.

In the state of consciousness the human soul knows that there is the possibility to be a Master, but in

---

8. Torkom Saraydarian, *Challenge For Discipleship* (Sedona, AZ: Aquarian Educational Group, 1986).

actuality he is not a Master yet. Whenever he **becomes** a Master, he is a Master at that level. His **beingness** is equal to a Master.

We are told that the consciousness on any plane must reach **four** levels ahead of our beingness in order to provide conditions to cause transformation in our beingness or actualization. When the beingness moves ahead toward the consciousness, the consciousness moves still further forward, and it expands more and more and makes beingness follow its lead.

What do we mean when we say that the consciousness moves ahead of beingness? To give a very simple example, let us say that you think and eventually create the theory and then the blueprint of a new kind of computer. But this blueprint, although it works in your mental realm, is not yet actualized. When it is actualized and is ready to operate on the physical plane, it is analogous to beingness.

But after such an actualization, the consciousness seeks further discoveries or penetrates higher levels of thoughts and ideas and creates a new blueprint, a new computer, and so on. Exactly in the same manner, our consciousness and aspiration do the job of vanguards, and beingness follows.

Consciousness is like one foot moving ahead of the other to pull the other foot ahead. In reality, consciousness and beingness are two parts of the human soul. Your beingness is found on any plane where you are not only conscious, but where you also can actualize the knowledge gained in any particular plane—on that plane or on lower planes. Through consciousness you are aware. Through beingness you actualize your awareness.

Cosmic Physical Plane

Divine Plane	1	1
	2	2
	3	3
	4	4
	5	5
	6	6
	7	7
Monadic Plane	8	1
	9	2
	10	3
	11	4
	12	5
	13	6
	14	7
Atmic Plane	15	1
	16	2
	17	3
	18	4
	19	5
	20	6
	21	7
Buddhic Plane	22	1
	23	2
	24	3
	25	4
	26	5
	27	6
	28	7
Mental Plane	29	1
	30	2
	31	3
	32	4
	33	5
	34	6
	35	7
Astral Plane	36	1
	37	2
	38	3
	39	4
	40	5
	41	6
	42	7
Physical Plane	43	1
	44	2
	45	3
	46	4
	47	5
	48	6
	49	7

Let us take human evolution. The above chart shows the make-up of the Cosmic Physical Plane, which is the first Plane of the Seven Cosmic Planes. In the Cosmic Physical Plane are seven subplanes. Each subplane is made up of seven levels, totaling forty-nine. The number seven level is the lowest point of each subplane.

Metaphysically speaking, to pull the human soul up from the lowest physical levels, his consciousness must rise to the second subplane of the physical plane, so that the human soul moves out from the seventh level of the physical plane to the sixth level.

When the consciousness reaches the third level of the mental plane, the beingness of man focuses itself on the lowest level of the mental plane.

When the consciousness moves further to the sixth level of the Intuitional (Buddhic) Plane, beingness reaches to the third level of the mental plane—where the fusion with the Solar Angel takes place.

The Fifth Initiation begins when the person's beingness operates on the seventh level of the Atmic Plane.

The Ageless Wisdom says that spiritual progress becomes possible when the third level substance is released into a given vehicle.

Each plane is composed of substance that has seven levels. Each level has its own atomic construction of various magnitudes. The higher we go on levels, the more powerful and rhythmic are the atoms of that level.

The third level substance provides such a rhythm that it can transmute the lower levels and synthesize them with itself.

The Seventh Initiation is achieved when the awareness penetrates into the third level of the Divine Plane, and beingness actualizes itself on the seventh level of the Divine Plane. Resurrected Ones are Those who bring Their beingness to the third level of the Divine Plane, during which Their consciousness already operates in the sixth subplane of the Cosmic Astral Plane.

Advancement on the ladder of evolution is achieved by expanding your consciousness, then growing toward it with your beingness. Your beingness is transformed immediately when your consciousness moves ahead. The Ageless Wisdom is dedicated to the expansion and elevation of the human consciousness. Expansions of consciousness cannot be continued unless beingness moves ahead. In a sense, unless beingness actually moves ahead, consciousness has no chance to expand further.

It is interesting to note that the third level of the physical plane is the first level at which beingness awakens as a physical existence. The same thing happens on the astral, mental, and higher planes. For example, on the third level of the mental plane, beingness becomes conscious of itself as a mental entity. This means that consciousness must be raised to the higher mental plane in order to come to this realization.

Let us say that we speak to you about a Treasure City of which you have never heard, and we tell you that the streets in this city run from east to west and from north to south, and then we tell you about its theaters, spiritual centers, and libraries. Does it make any difference if we are letting you know that the city exists, even if we do not give you all the exact information and details of that city? Would you prefer to remain unaware of the city until we give you perfect and exact details of it?

The fact is that the city will be there, and by the time you find that city, all of the details will be different from the present descriptions!

Who, then, will think of success in the Subtle World, if it is not permissible to speak and think? The Teaching which does not know the Subtle World does not serve as a guide, because earthly existence is not an hundredth part of the life in the Subtle World.[9]

Wisdom and Beingness

Those who want to study the Ageless Wisdom manifesting in the seven fields of human endeavor must bear in mind the following points:

1. Their goal is not only to collect wisdom but also to assimilate it.

2. Their goal is not only to assimilate it but also to practice it in their own daily life.

Assimilation and practice of Wisdom build your soul. Thus your real beingness comes into existence.

For example, you learn about compassion, trust, gratitude, sacrifice, and you can write wonderful articles or books, and you can give fascinating lectures about them—but if you are not a compassionate, trustworthy person, or if you do not carry the spirit of gratitude in your heart, if you are not sacrificial, you

9. Agni Yoga Society, *Heart* (New York: Agni Yoga Society, 1934), para. 329.

have no beingness; you have no actualization. This is like eating food without digesting it.

Those who want to study the Ageless Wisdom must try to be real, to be actualized, and to be solid human beings in their own field.

One day my father, speaking about a person, said, "He is a living book of wisdom."

I thought much about that expression. A person must be the embodiment of that which he believes. Your wisdom and you must be one. That is what beingness is. Beingness advances and progresses in digesting Wisdom and living that Wisdom through all relationships.

According to the Ageless Wisdom we have seven bodies in which the soul—us—shines like a star.

All the seven bodies are a complete mechanism in the hand of the human soul, but he cannot really use all of them until he expands his consciousness and beingness and climbs the ladder of evolution from plane to plane, from the lower body to a higher one, continually refining and building these bodies according to the demand of his expanding consciousness and the need of the environment.

For example, on the physical plane he develops the brain, nervous system, glands, chakras, and senses. On the emotional plane he develops sensitivity to the feelings and emotions, plus the seven astral senses and astral centers. In the mental body he develops the power of thinking, plus the mental centers and senses and the "Temple not made by hands."

In higher astral bodies he builds more refined psychic devices to communicate with still higher spheres. We must remember that one of the major goals of the Ageless Wisdom is to make a person, a group, a race, have closer and more advanced communication with all that exists in order to reach its purpose.

The Ageless Wisdom requests that we learn to think in abstract and concrete terms simultaneously, and be idealistic and practical at the same time.

The Ageless Wisdom is not satisfied with our thinking ability, but requests the development of the heart, with compassion, inclusiveness, gratitude, and with other virtues. For the Ageless Wisdom, even these are not enough. It requests from us to prove our mental capacities and heart qualities with our service. The bigger the field of our service, the higher the number of those who are benefited through our service, the greater will be our speed on the path.

The reward of the student of the Ageless Wisdom is the increase of his labor in an expanding field of service.

It is through thinking and through the heart and through labor that man will increase in wisdom, beauty, understanding, and beingness in the field of his chosen service.

Chapter Four

Fanaticism And Faithfulness

Some people wonder if faithfulness to the Teaching is akin to fanaticism. The answer is that they are two totally different approaches.

Faithfulness to the Teaching is based on the belief that the accepted and taught Teaching is going to be carried on as it was given by the original Source.

Faithfulness to the Teaching does not attack the other forms of beliefs, the followers of which consider their own beliefs beneficial for many people, but faithfulness to the Teaching rejects all those elements in other beliefs that are sectarian, superstitious, separative, and charged with the spirit of fanaticism.

Faithfulness to the Teaching is inclusive. It recognizes the precious gems in other beliefs or philosophies and makes them a part of the Teaching.

Every truth, every wisdom, every true revelation, no matter in what form or from what origin, is a part of the Teaching.

Fanaticism is the imposition of a set of beliefs on others, proclaiming that all else is against the Truth. A fanatic thinks that his beliefs are the only way to achieve perfection. Generally, fanaticism carries with it a few ugly companions—anger, violence, imposition, treason, malice, and slander. Fanaticism uses them all.

A fanatic is always closed to new revelations or discoveries. He is attached to whatever he has, and he cannot expand his mental prison.

In the case of faithfulness, the person has pure discrimination and does not allow any faulty teaching to enter in. Faithfulness is responsible for guarding many treasures given by Great Ones throughout ages, such as these, among others:

— *Vedas*

— *Puranas*

— *Upanishads*

— *Ramayana*

— *Mahabharata*

— Teachings of Buddha

— Teachings of Jesus

— *Kaballa*

The Teaching has survived until today because the guardians of these philosophies did not mix them with the teachings of those who were far below the consciousness of Those Who gave these Teachings.

Faithfulness looks for the pure Teaching. It believes that the Teaching can increase and grow in volume and dimension by those or through those who have a pure understanding of the Teaching.

In this case, new additions to the Teaching will always be in harmony with the Teaching given by the Great Ones, and no contradictions will be found. There will possibly be a deepening and expanding of some of the fundamental ideas and principles.

Fanaticism cannot grow because it makes the following declarations:

1. All that I know is the last word, and it is all that can be given.

2. All the rest is wrong.

3. All must deny their path and follow my beliefs, or else they must be persecuted in various ways.

When a person studies the Teaching, it is very important for the first five to seven years of study to keep the consciousness of the student very clear and in certainty until his consciousness grows and his sense of discrimination ripens. Before this, a mixed formulation or presentation can cause great damage to the mind of the student and eventually make him confused or paralyzed.

When a student of Wisdom develops discrimination and intuition, he must be allowed to approach other faiths, philosophies, or religions to see how he can find a common denominator between them and try to develop such techniques by which he can translate other faiths in a way that they do not contradict the one that he has or had.

The attitude of faithfulness is a search for truth and fact, no matter where they are found. To be able to pursue such a search, one must really believe that his faith is based upon a real foundation.

Faithfulness gradually turns into an all-inclusive search for Truth. Such a person no longer belongs to his church, philosophy, group, and so on, but he belongs to the Truth. Such a person fits in with all religions, in all philosophies and sciences because he is able to sense and see the essence of things instead of their phenomena.

To be able to achieve such a state of consciousness, the beginner, no matter of what faith, must be protected against the penetration of other religious beliefs or philosophies until he develops a foundation in his own faith. The mechanism of the mind can be damaged very easily if, for example, a child is taken from his environment of faith and beliefs and then filled with other presentations of the Teaching. At such an early stage, only contradiction and confusion will be created in him, nothing else.

All great Teachings contain Cosmic Principles and Laws, and in essence all agree. It is fatal to fish for people and force them to change their religion.

Once the mind is confused, the person will reject, misuse, or distort the faith, religion, or philosophy that the forceful one is presenting to him. The person will also reject his own faith and be without any moral or spiritual support and foundation for many incarnations. Such a crime must not be committed for the sake of adding to the membership of a group or increasing its income.

It is true that one can be a faithful fanatic. This is worse than one who is only a fanatic. A faithful fanatic tries to create every kind of intellectual game to show that his belief cannot be surpassed and that it is the only one, from beginning to end. Is there any bigger crime than the denial that in the future no one will surpass the level of the person who is the source of a faith? How can one imagine that the mind, working through humanity, will not develop to such a degree that any past achievements of the mind will be considered elementary or even childish? How can one put such blocks on the path of eternal and infinite progress by using dogmas and doctrines which prevent people from passing beyond them? Can you imagine anyone saying, "Please accept my conclusions and observations as truth forever and do not try to penetrate deeper or have more inclusive observations on life as a whole?"

There are such people in all fields of human endeavor. Faithfulness, however, sees all of these comedies and searches for purer and purer principles in the Universe.

Fanaticism persecutes individuals, groups, and nations. When anyone is persecuted for his religious beliefs, he eventually absorbs all the hatred, terror, and anger that were directed toward him, and he turns them into the force of revenge. Years later, or after many lives, these persecuted and hated ones become the enemies of humanity or the enemies of the nation in which they were persecuted. Humanity or that nation will have to pay for all the pain, suffering, and various kinds of damage that were inflicted on the persecuted ones. The pure Teaching emphasizes the principle of harmlessness because any harm caused will return to those who caused it.

In true faithfulness, the principle of harmlessness should be the controlling factor in all relationships. Faithfulness is often condemned by those who like to swim in "muddy lakes" and enjoy conflicting situations because they do not have faith in either side of the conflict. They are there only to secure their own personal interests.

How can we condemn a mathematician who follows the principles of pure mathematics, of pure measures and pure numbers? In the field of mathematics and science, people will not accept any faulty numbers, calculations, and measures. Why, then, do we not exercise the same practice in the field of the Teaching, in the field of faith and beliefs?

There are right things and wrong things in every field. Why would adherence to what is right be condemned in any field?

Is it not possible that the difference between right and wrong beliefs, or the value of mixed beliefs, could be targeted or determined by an intelligent mind and by the fruits and effects of those beliefs in society? There should be a measure by which we can discover if a belief is pure, mixed, or impure.

Christ gave one measure when He said, "By their fruits you will know them." Lord Buddha advised His disciples to develop detachment. Mohammed taught self-forgetfulness and surrender. Moses taught to obey the Will of the Most High. Using these statements, can people build a device to measure future revelations?

There are certain risks in accepting a person into the Teaching.

1. The person may be a hindrance or disturbing factor if he does not deepen his faith in the Teaching by his study and practice of it.

2. The person may be frustrated when he sees senior members still harboring hatred, jealousy, ego, and vanity.

3. The person may feel so privileged to be a member that he loses the desire to strive. Those who do not strive become trouble-

makers in the particular group and disturb the peace, serenity, and integrity of that group.

These three conditions must not be allowed to develop in any student. To avoid these risks, every student in a group must do the following:

1. Study, meditate, and serve.

2. Not look at how others act. Look only at his ideal.

3. Feel that he always needs to change and progress. That is how he can be a good member who brings light and energy to the group.

Fundamentalism is not faithfulness. Fundamentalism is a belief based on certain foundations which were laid two thousand to seven thousand years ago. Tradition, or the writings that were given long ago, had a different meaning then than our current translations and we erroneously tend to accept our translations as the solid truth.

Even if these foundations are understood as they were before, they will not necessarily meet all the various needs and demands of contemporary humanity. Human life is progressive, and on each step of its progress it has new needs, new keys to solve problems, new demands, and new aspirations.

Foundations are important, but one must not single out the foundation of his room for consideration and then deny the foundation of the whole building. To find the real foundation of a single room, one must find the foundation of the entire building, or else he can be misled. The foundation of the entire building is called the Ageless Wisdom. **The foundation of the Ageless**

Wisdom is Light—Light which is ever-progressive in Its expressions and manifestations.

Faithfulness to the Teaching is dedication to pure Light in all manifestations or expressions of the Light. Fanaticism is a blind adherence to one portion of the foundation and a declaration that this portion is the foundation of the past, present, and future. Usually such a portion of an entire foundation is a stone which was deserted by the builders and buried because of its uselessness.

True fundamentalism is faithfulness to the foundations of the Teaching, but it turns into fanaticism when it thinks that its foundation is all that exists. One cannot be a true fundamentalist unless he includes the foundations of all religious wisdom and science. It is here that fanaticism melts away in the recognition that besides the hut of a person's individualized religion and beliefs there is a super-structure with "many mansions."

Fundamentalists fall into fanaticism when they do not stand on the foundation of the entire, ever-growing, and ever-expanding tower of Wisdom.

Fundamentalism and fanaticism are separative, and separatism is the root of all hatred and fear. That is why everywhere in the world even the "worshipers" of the one God fight against each other to annihilate one another.

Under these conditions, religious wars and hatred will increase and will create more instability in the world, causing economic disaster. In past ages, we used to live far apart from each other, secluded in valleys and mountains. Today, the world is almost one; we are all close neighbors. We can damage each other permanently if we pursue our old-fashioned separatisms.

As nations and races of people are getting closer and closer in their physical existence, it is imperative that people develop acceptance through understanding each other's foundation. It is through intelligent acceptance that right human relationships will prevail and will lead us toward unity.

In the past, humanity created its tools for survival. We also must create tools to build our own survival ships in this age. Old tools cannot produce the sophisticated mental equipment we now need. We need new tools to meet the needs of a new life.

Old tools, old keys, old belief systems, traditions, religions, and philosophies can help us know how people used to think in the past and what problems they tried to solve. We must closely examine these tools with reverence to understand them and, if necessary, create new ones to solve our new problems.

Centuries from now, if an inclusive generation arises, they will try to learn from each "tool" we created, to see why we created it and to see how much that tool was helpful for our survival and happiness. It is these all-inclusive generations that will determine whether or not our tools were made for survival or for self-destruction.

Chapter Five

Dangers And The Ageless Wisdom

There is great danger in studying the Ageless Wisdom without applying it to our lives. In reading and studying it, we build certain patterns in the system of our mind which, like a network of electrical wires, must be grounded through practical application.

If we do not practically apply the Ageless Wisdom, it becomes a separate entity in our mental plane which prevents the mind from assimilating new ideas and new energies. To establish the flow of energy in our entire system, grounding is necessary, or else the electricity will remain where it is in the mental plane.

The Ageless Wisdom puts a person in contact with higher, fiery spheres. One can protect himself from these fiery currents only by providing an outlet into practical life through his thoughts, words, and actions. Crystallized teaching in the mental sphere does not allow the human soul to grow. Growth of the soul is possible only when knowledge of the Ageless Wisdom is made practical.

The human soul learns the Teaching only through the process of actualization. The human soul grows when the expansion of its consciousness is parallel to its beingness. Beingness is achieved only through practical application of the Teaching. If there is no application, the soul is divided in two. One part is occupied with the Teaching; the other part is enslaved by the pleasures of the bodies.

Hypocrisy is a disease of a split ego. The person does not appear in his outer relationships the way he is inside. Such a cleavage creates great pressure on the whole mechanism of the person, causing various disorders in his mechanism due to the irregular and contradictory currents flowing from the human soul.

There also occurs the disease of abstraction of the mind when the mental body partially withdraws from the brain and occupies itself only with the ideas of the Teaching. In such a case, the person becomes confused, scattered in mind, unreal and impractical, as if he were living in a dream. This brings numerous complications into his family, social, and business life. A person's judgment decreases, and his ability to calculate becomes disturbed. In this condition, he faces defeat and failure.

The Teaching draws a tremendous amount of energy from higher values which is often trapped by a person's glamors, illusions, ego, vanity, blind urges, and drives. Very soon these elements grow out of proportion and make him feel like he is drowning in a flood of pleasures, stupidity, and obscenity from which he cannot free himself.

This is why we need a Teacher who can feed us only that which we can digest or apply in life. Reading the Teaching and hearing lectures about it may pump a person's vanity and ego to such a degree that he becomes arrogant and self-centered. Fanaticism and bigotry increase, and he turns into a servant of separatism.

Such a person acts as if he were special—"chosen" or "saved"—and he looks down on others as if they had no right to live. This creates a tendency to exploit people. When such a feeling begins to appear in a person, his striving toward perfection stops and he begins to work and live as a show-off. This phenomenon is referred to as "living for the sake of the surface."

When a person studies the Teaching, he attracts powerful entities around him which stimulate his aura and bring all his latent "bugs" to the surface of his life. "Bugs" are deep-seated and suppressed

- vices

- hatreds

- desires

- cravings

- guilt

When these things surface, a person needs a Teacher to help him, and he needs to observe strict obedience and follow the guidance of the Teacher. If he does not follow this advice and eliminate the rubbish floating on the surface of his aura, the bright and beautiful entities depart and he attracts evil entities, destructive forces, and possessors who come and slowly settle among the rubbish. From this moment on, a person becomes a haunted house and his own destruction ensues.

If we study the Teaching and do not assimilate it through

- meditation

- practice

- service

we slowly become the enemy of the Teaching and the Teacher, and dark forces use us to destroy the Teaching—either by making us poor examples of the Teaching so that others around us come to abhor the Teaching, or by directly making us destructive agents in groups or in committees.

When the Teaching is read but not assimilated and practiced, it builds a wall between the lower mind and the higher mind which prevents us for ages from passing to Higher Realms. Such a state make the wheel of incarnation continue to turn in painful existences. This state is referred to as being trapped in the lower mind. Multitudes of people are trapped in this way.

In ancient literature and scriptures, we are told that the Teaching is fire.

- It burns.

- It purifies.

- It transforms.

It burns if the person is identified with his trash. It purifies if he sees his faults, errors, and mistakes, hates them and then aspires toward higher achievement. It transforms when he cooperates with it by making real, sincere efforts to change his nature by the light of the Teaching.

Chapter Six

Reaction To The Teaching

The Teaching is the accumulated Wisdom of the ages. It is the accumulated experiences that awakened human souls had throughout ages. It is the accumulated revelations given to them from the Higher Worlds.

The Teaching is the result of contact with the pure Light by these collective souls and the translation of that Light in terms of progressive principles, laws, and standards.[1]

Great Souls adapted the Teaching to the seven fields of human endeavor[2] and brought greater and greater illumination into those fields, subjectively building a network of harmony among them which will be slowly revealed in the ages to come. Thus, the Teaching on the human level is divided into seven fields with seven goals in order to raise the standard level of human life, to make it a progressive, healthy organization, and to see the purpose toward which life is destined to lead humanity.

The first goal is to create right human relations. The Teaching reveals to human beings how to cooperate with each other and how to establish right human relations all over the world.

---

1. For further information regarding the source of the Teaching, please refer to *The Psyche and Psychism* by Torkom Saraydarian (Agoura, CA: Aquarian Educational Group, 1981), Chapters 41, 42, 43.

2. Politics, Education, Communication, the Arts, Science, Religion, Economics.

Second, the Teaching explains how to gain victory over our lower self, over the mechanical part of ourselves, and act as self-conscious and self-determined human beings.

Third, the Teaching gives the whole science of how to enlighten people.

Fourth, the Teaching gives a system of knowledge which enables people to contact the Higher Worlds. The Teaching says that the Higher Worlds are those spheres where there is greater light and more highly enlightened souls. These spheres are the abode of the ideas, visions, and beauty with which human beings must communicate.

Fifth, the Teaching contains all those principles and laws through which we can develop the sense of synthesis and create synthesis within ourselves, within a group, within a nation, and within humanity as a whole.

Sixth, the Teaching emphasizes that everyone of us must follow the five-pointed star of Beauty, Goodness, Righteousness, Joy, and Freedom in order to have a healthy, happy, prosperous, creative, and heroic life.

Seventh, the Teaching says that we must get rid of our ego and vanity in order to be able to understand the Teaching, to assimilate it, and to apply it to life.

If we keep such goals in mind and strive in one, two, or in all fields to spread these ideas, we are in the Teaching. The Teaching penetrates into our soul when we, with right motives, work and dedicate ourselves to the upliftment of the human race.

Every true server sooner or later finds the pure Teaching, meets those who teach the Teaching, and experiences a life transformed through the Teaching. But this does not proceed smoothly. The Teaching evokes severe resistance which accumulates and turns into terrible difficulties. A Teacher says, "At times we did not have a place to stay." This Teacher once asked Urusvati:

> *Urusvati, can you name even one sister or brother who has not been subjected to torture and persecution in earthly life? Truly none can be named. Each act of heroism invites persecution. Combat with darkness is unavoidable, and the waves of chaos will engulf the bold fighter. Yet each touchstone only testifies to the invincibility of the spirit. There were those who were burned at the stakes, those crucified, those beheaded, those strangled, those killed by beasts, sold into slavery, those poisoned, those cast into prisons; in short, all tortures have been endured in order to test one's strength.*

> *It should not be thought that the expansion of consciousness is achieved without a struggle. Each one who wishes to serve Us knows that he will have to endure the assaults of darkness.*[3]

Such phenomena are observed all over the world. In all departments of human endeavor, people react to those who bring new ideas, new visions, and new goals.

First of all, when someone speaks to us about the Teaching and about what the Teaching expects from us, we feel a reaction from our lower self. The reason for this reaction is that the crystallized habits, emotions, and thoughtforms feel that they are under at-

---

3. Agni Yoga Society, *Supermundane*. Unpublished writings of Helena Roerich.

tack. It is not easy to break our habits, our mechanical responses and reactions, our ways of thinking, not only because they are set in certain patterns but also because they are associated with our immediate families, churches, businesses, and traditions. Yet, nothing can change within us without changing all those things with which we are associated. This is often painful for ourselves and for others.

For example, the Teaching suggests that we not eat meat, drink alcohol, or smoke. When you decide to abstain from these things, your friends and family will probably wonder if you have lost your mind. This creates family and social problems, and sometimes in changing yourself you may lose your family, friends, and job. Sometimes you even lose your church, if the people in your church see that you are really entering the path of transformation. Thus we can see that the Teaching not only creates reactions from your lower self, from your habits, from your crystallized emotions, beliefs, traditions, and religions but also from your environment and everyone in it!

For an advanced human being, his family, group or society becomes like his lower self. Just as his lower self reacts to the Teaching, similarly and for almost the same reasons his family, group, and society attack and react to him.

Our families, groups, parties, societies, and so on construct barriers on our path when we seriously begin to follow the Teaching and carry out the disciplines that are presented to us by the Teaching. Reactions start first in the field where we are most active. If we are bringing in new political ideas and if we are talking about peace, world unity, cooperation, and disarmament, we will experience severe reactions from various layers of people in that field and associated fields.

If we are in the religious field and we are trying to introduce the ideas of the Teaching, we will find severe reactions which may lead us to crucifixion, to the stake, or into a knife or bullet that terminates our earthly life. Any advanced thinker eventually becomes a sore point in the society in which he lives and a point of worship for future generations.

The only crime Jesus committed was to bring in new ideas which could lead humanity into a greater happiness, but He was crucified. His disciples were also killed, as well as a great majority of His followers. The spiritual fire in those who survived slowly dimmed until that fire was finally exterminated around 350 A.D. The followers of Jesus began to survive because they no longer evoked any sort of real resistance.

The resistance slowly died out, and the Christians began to live as others before them had lived—in great palaces, in great temples, in great positions and wealth. Worldly interests swallowed them up.

Whenever a Teaching does not expand, it turns into dogma, doctrine, ritual, and organizations; its spirit dies and the shell remains. The only way to keep the fire burning is to provide new spiritual fuel for it by having steady contact with the original Source of the Teaching.

Great Teachers do not give the Teaching all at once. The Teaching is composed of a series of revelations which come one after the other in cycles, like the waves of the ocean. The reason that They cannot give the Teaching all at once is that They want us to receive the Teaching, then live it and expand our consciousness in order to be able to receive the next revelation. But if we crystallize and accept the Teaching as formulas, words, dogmas, doctrines, and rituals, we will reject the new wave of the Teaching when it begins to hit our shores.

No religion or Teaching can be final. It changes because of our growth and expanding consciousness. It changes because of new challenges, new needs, and new cycles of incoming energies. It changes because of the new development of humanity.

Religions and ideologies are just like human beings. They have a Higher Self and a lower self. The Higher Self is like an increasing light and an expanding plane. The lower self is the organizational, form side of the ideology. If the lower self of the ideology or religion cannot change, expand, and reform under the pressures of the Higher Self, there is reaction; the lower self refuses to accept the Higher Self and lives by itself. This is how great ideologies eventually crystallize and lose their transforming power.

I once gave one of my books to a woman who then called me in the middle of the night to say, "This book is a great delight. I feel as if I were able to fly once again." I gave the same book to another who brought it back, saying, "I do not want this book; it does not agree with my opinions." Certain people cannot expand and do not want to progress. This is true in all seven fields of human endeavor, in all countries, in all nations.

Let us take each field of human endeavor in relation to the Teaching:

1. Politics. In the political field, the Teaching clearly stands for inclusiveness, progress, sensitivity, unity, and freedom. Those who react to the Teaching emphasize separatism, self-interest, domination, totalitarianism. These two sides are fighting against one another. If the Teaching wins, the planet will be safe. If the Teaching loses, we will lose humanity.

2. Education. In the field of education, the Teaching reveals, enlightens, and spreads light for the Common Good. The reaction to the Teaching educates in order to promote self-interest and competition. Which side will win?

3. Communication. In the field of communication, the Teaching says to spread Beauty, Goodness, Righteousness, Freedom, and Joy all over the world. The reaction to the Teaching demands excitement, tries to distort, lie, manipulate, and make money through the news.

There is a clash between these two, and we see how every day the media builds a world nourished by crime, fear, vice, and destruction.

I once wrote to my Teacher and said, "Life is becoming very frightening. I am distributing works by various authors related to the Teaching, and, by doing so, I am creating many enemies in society, in my church, and even among my relatives."

"Very good, very good," replied my Teacher. "Now you are proving that you are becoming a disciple. A disciple, if alive and active, must create reactions. Reactions will unveil your enemies and will keep you alive and progressively striving. Do not have fear. Reactions sooner or later consume themselves as they are not based on truth."

One does not need to plan to create reaction. Reaction will be there when you start growing toward the light. Of course, in addition to reaction, you will also have responses from those who are ready and open enough to receive your light. These are your co-workers who, when they join with you, will evoke greater reactions from those who are afraid that their interests will be endangered because of your Teaching. Your co-workers will move the wheel of the society forward—and that will be your joy.

4. Art. The Teaching says that art must be the manifestation of the Inner Glory, that its intention is to release the Inner Glory in others. Programmed, reactionary people say that art can be used to exploit, to manipulate, to stir up the chaos existing in the lower desires, blind urges, and drives. You can see how such "ideas" are propagated in movies and books.

5. Science. In the field of science the Teaching says, "Let knowledge belong to everyone to heal cleavages and lead humanity into prosperity, health, and happiness."

The Teaching instructs us not to pollute nature: the air, the atmosphere, the waters of the Earth, or its soil. The Teaching says, instead, that we must use science to clean nature. There is nothing wrong in this statement to a person who is sane. But, of course, this statement is wrong to a person whose interests are at stake if pollution is stopped, if insecticides are not sold, and if poison-producing factories are closed.

The Teaching is nothing but a clash between what is sane and what is insane. Already we are having very serious problems with the ozone layer. Humanity will see that the carpet is being pulled out from under its feet. It will soon be too late to do anything creative.

6. Religion. In the field of religion the Teaching says, "Religion is the experience of contact with the Most High." No matter how much you visit your places of worship and read your scriptures, you are not a religious person if you have no real contact with the

Most High and if you have not renounced your will for His Will.

Those who react say, "We need dogma, doctrine, ritual, ceremony, positions, control, fanaticism. Our scriptures are better than the holy books of others. We are going to heaven. . . so, certainly, others are going to hell!"

7. Economics. In the field of economics, the Teaching says that all resources of Mother Nature belong to everyone, everywhere, and that these resources must be shared with all nations. What a great change would enter into our consciousness if we understood this Teaching and lived for it.

On the other hand, the reactionary party says, "Our resources belong to us. We can use them to dominate and subdue other nations. We can manipulate and exploit others to increase new forms of pleasure for ourselves." In Atlantean times, people thought in the same way—and the flood engulfed all that they had.

Average people create reactions in society because of their crimes, stupidities, ignorance, and ugliness. Most of our laws have been created to protect people from such persons or even to protect the person from himself. The disciples of the world create reactions because of their beauty, goodness, righteousness, joy, freedom, solemnity, pure sense of responsibility, and wisdom.

The greater the reactions of crystallized people, the sooner they will surrender to the forces of light, beauty, and joy. That is why every disciple must be daring and courageous enough to live the Teaching with the intention of serving humanity.

We have reactions, also, from within us. Our blind urges and drives fight the Teaching. Our glamors and illusions fight the Teaching. Our crystallized ideas, illusions, ego, vanity, and separatism fight the Teaching. All of these fight because they know that they will lose their control of us if the Teaching wins, but the more they fight, the more the Higher Self conquers them through the Teaching.

So, the first cause of reaction against the Teaching comes from your lower self and from those who relate to your lower self. Either your higher consciousness is fighting against your blind urges, drives, glamors, and illusions, or you are very happy with yourself. If you are very happy with yourself, you are already a dead person. But if conflict begins within you and you decide to cooperate with your Higher Self, then you are a warrior on behalf of humanity. Can you do this? If you cannot, then you are going to be a slave to your habits, blind urges, and drives, and you will never work in cooperation with your Higher Self. You have lost the battle.

Create a battle within yourself. If you are really happy with yourself, there is no hope. When people come and say, "We know it; we are," the trash can is waiting for them. Once you start fighting your vanity and ego and say, "Ego, I do not like you," it will scream to death and say to you, "Why don't you like me? It was I who made you great. It was I who gave you a chance to overcome people and control them. It was I who helped you to exploit." If you can find one, two, or three mistakes that you really do not like in yourself, then you are on the Path now.

Make a list of twenty-five points which say what you want to be and check them. If sincerity is number one on your list, ask yourself if you are sincere. If you are not sincere, start fighting against the insincerity within your nature and you will see the results. Not only will you fight against yourself, but you will fight against those who cooperate with your lower self against your Higher Self. That is why the Great Ones say that the Teaching brings conflict. Also, it is the secret behind what Christ said: "I came to bring a sword, not peace." The sword is the symbol of pure discrimination in the fight for the sake of the Higher Self.

The lower self is against Beauty, Goodness, Righteousness, Joy, and Freedom. For example, you go home and find your teen-age son watching television, and you say, "I need you to help me carry things in from the car." But he says, "I am tired. I want to go to sleep." Such a person is serving his lower self. But if he immediately jumps up and says, "Mom, what can I do to help? Let me clean; let me wash; let me carry things for you," he is obeying his Higher Self.

There is a condition in our nature which is very zoo-like. We have collected wild animals, good and bad animals, and have stored them in our physical, emotional, and mental natures. They will all sleep peacefully as long as they are fed and cared for. But once we become a servant of light, they will start howling from every corner of our nature, "Why is he against us? The light hurts our eyes! Discipline, meditation, and solemnity are hurting our stomach!" When we listen to their howling, we become like them. If we do not listen to them, they surface one by one and we can annihilate them. This was explained in the *Bhagavad Gita*[4] in a very philosophical way. The *Gita* is a story of the battle between the lower self and the Higher Self, and in it Krishna gives ways to conquer

---

4. Torkom Saraydarian, trans., *The Bhagavad Gita* (Agoura, CA: Aquarian Educational Group, 1974).

the lower self through the Supreme Teaching of battle.

People think that solitude helps to conquer the lower self. It depends on the person's level of understanding and energy. If a person is weak and flooded with glamors and illusions, blind urges and drives, solitude will not help him. It is better for him to have a friend around who bugs him so that he starts awakening. If he goes instead into solitude for two or three days, he becomes happy and remains on the same level of consciousness. That is why we say that groups are necessary. Groups are boiling pots: either you survive or you degenerate. When people enter a group, their vanity, ego, and vices surface. Their good qualities also manifest and grow.

It is very good to create conflict in others; in fact, if you do not, you are dead. Those who do not affect the lives of others are people who are in their graves.

Once you overcome something in battle, you do not need to repeat it in future incarnations.

Living with others develops the sense of responsibility so that you learn to live not only for yourself but also for other people—and in such a way that your presence makes them advance, expand, and become more beautiful.

One day Christ called his disciple Peter and said, "Go listen to what the people are saying about Me." He wanted to know what the reactions and responses were to His Teaching so that He could change His voltage accordingly. We do not do the same thing. We live in a tower and think that we are a king. Go see what the coyotes are thinking about you.

For example, your lower nature may say, "Steal." But when you check with your Higher Self and say,

"You know, my lower nature wants to steal, but I don't want to steal," then you start fighting with your lower self. The thoughts, emotions, and actions of the lower self are the first cause of reaction to the Teaching.

The second cause of reaction to the Teaching comes from your body. Your body as a whole reacts to the Teaching. The Teaching puts certain disciplines over your physical nature—upon your sex habits, sleeping habits, eating habits—and the body does not like such pressures until it is slowly transformed and sublimated.

The third cause of reaction to the Teaching appears when the person is transformed by the Teaching or when he becomes a sore spot or a source of agitation in society. People reject him, just as the lower self rejects the Higher Self and just as the programmed self rejects the new Teaching.

In conclusion, we may say that whatever we think, speak, and do programs our mind, our emotional body, and our physical body. It does not take long to see that our programming is running the show. When we want to introduce a new thought, we feel the rejection of these three bodies. The more crystallized they are, the stronger will be the reaction. Similarly, the stronger the new thinking, the more fierce will be the battle within our nature.

These three reactions on individual levels also have corresponding reactions or similar reactions in larger groups of people.

Some people are so crystallized that any new Teaching cracks them, confuses them, and even makes them sick. It affects their thinking mechanism, their speech mechanism, and their action mechanism. The new way of thinking, speaking, and acting creates disturbances in them because they cannot easily adapt themselves to a higher frequency.

Chapter Seven

Certainty

The Ageless Wisdom creates certainty in your soul. It reveals the Purpose of life and gives you the Plan of how to achieve that Purpose. It shows you the infinite possibilities available to expand your consciousness and see the entire creation in a holistic way. It tells you about yourself; it tells you what you are and what you can be. It explains the meaning of your successive lives. It does not leave you in darkness or in confusion.

Those who follow the Ageless Wisdom live longer, healthier, and more balanced lives because they have certainty in their consciousness. They live in balance with the whole of Nature. They die with joy and with the determination to carry on their evolution toward Higher Spheres. The blows of life and the failures cannot discourage them. They stand up and follow the path of light and joy. They pay their karma gracefully and stand against the cold winds and blizzards of snow with a smiling face.

Certainty makes a person fearless, courageous, and daring. He knows what he is doing and why he is doing it. It creates balance between the centers, and their relationships become harmonious. This brings energy, joy, and health.

Certainty in a person evokes trust and confidence from others; people believe in him. They feel that he is not a changeable person but has a firm, solid character. The development of this trust makes a man of certainty help and serve others and makes others heed his guidance.

Religion gives people a certain degree of certainty. That is why the Ageless Wisdom discourages us from forcing our own religion on others or trying to convert people, imposing our beliefs by force. To the Ageless Wisdom, all true religions are facets of the same stream of Teaching which have been given to people according to their need, character, and environment.

Sometimes severe psychological problems and deep-seated turbulences in the psyche of a person are created if he changes religions. However, the Ageless Wisdom encourages tolerance, compassion, and the search for the common denominator in all true religions.

Confusion is not constructive. Some think that they have to destroy others in order to break the crystallizations and prejudices in their minds. This action often leaves people in a desperate state. It is important to help an individual *within* the context of his own religion, helping him see the essence of his religion, its real foundations and goals, encouraging him to try to live according to the higher principles given in his religion. Those who truly live within the value structures and principles of their religion can always understand and cooperate with others.

Leadership, in essence, is certainty. No leadership can survive by wandering through confusion and uncertainty. Leaders must inspire and bestow certainty. If leaders cause political, ideological, and economic uncertainty, they will lose not only the trust of the people but also their own position and the health of the nation. In uncertainty, people tend to take anti-survival steps which lead to the degeneration of morals and principles. A person of uncertainty is shaky ground upon which no one can stand or build safely.

All our endeavors in life are attempts to create certainty:

- We want to secure our daily bread for tomorrow.
- We try to make ourselves prettier, more handsome.
- We try to dress well.
- We wear jewelry.
- We endeavor to have property or objects.
- We go to colleges and universities.
- We want to love and be loved.
- We try to trust and be trusted.
- We want to touch reality.
- We want to know that we are immortal.

All of these efforts are attempts to obtain certainty; we do this because no one can exist very long without certainty.

It is interesting to note that certainty is a progressive discovery. It is like finding something on the ground that, as you examine and touch it, you decide it has come from the ocean. You try to discover the part of it that is related to the ocean. Then, when you have fully discovered its relationship to the ocean, you see that some part of the object is related to the air—and you are led onto another field of exploration.

The reality of an object extends to all planes of the Cosmic Physical Plane. As you discover the same object on higher planes, your certainty increases; your radiation, ideas, and thoughts become more real, concrete, universal, and thus certain.

Faith is a substitute for, or a guarantee of, certainty. It is a feeling of certainty that you can be in contact with higher levels, a feeling for which there may not seem to be a logical explanation. This is why one must not attack the faith of others. Faith is an anchor for them without which they would be tossed into the ocean of uncertainty.

We can see faith from another viewpoint. Though faith can be the collective beliefs we have in our religion, faith is also an intuitive knowledge of that which exists beyond religion. It is the result of an experience, of a real contact.

Our certainty expands as our consciousness unfolds and penetrates into higher planes. Certainty, in its deeper meaning, is an increasing awareness of the Divine Self and of becoming that Self. The only certainty—the certainty which is the foundation of all certainties—is the Divine Self within. Unless we have an intuitive awareness of the existence of that Self, all other certainties will vanish.

Such a certainty of being the Higher Self is very important in the Subtle World—after we leave our body. Certainty is the feeling of identity. Unless we develop certainty about our identity, we will not be able to sail consciously on the ocean of the Subtle World, much less in the Higher Worlds.

You can observe how certainty in human relationships grows and brings a greater sense of reality. For example, you begin by loving a girl. She becomes more real when you touch her or kiss her. This reality grows when you touch her emotions, ideas, visions, values, and creativity. Thus, certainty is a multi-faceted diamond which you continually uncover, and as you uncover facet after facet, your joy increases in the increasing certainty and reality.

To repeat, certainty is the experience of reality. Reality exists on all levels simultaneously but not in the same magnitude. As a person proceeds toward the lower physical plane, reality becomes mixed with unreality. Reality becomes maya, illusion. But still, in this illusory world, the objects of this world give us a sense of certainty when we know or own them.

As we pass from one plane to a higher plane of existence, the lower plane reality and certainty disappear, and we realize that the objects of that plane were illusory. We experience this even for objects of the emotional and mental planes, if we are building the line of continuity of consciousness through which we can trace our relationships with the objects of the lower planes.

Let us imagine that you went to the mental plane after you left your body and that later you incarnated on the physical plane. If you were conscious on the etheric plane or higher planes for a long time, as you grow up on the physical plane, you will feel and know that most of the objects of the physical plane are unreal. You will never show attachment to them; neither will you kill, deceive, exploit, or manipulate people to own things that you know are unreal.

We can say that the faculty of discrimination grows as life after life we see what is real and what is unreal. The sense of discrimination always leads to certainty. Without the sense of discrimination, we are lost in confusion and uncertainty. When, through experience and discrimination, a person realizes the illusory nature of the objects of the world, he lives on that plane as a superior human being who guides people from the jungles of uncertainty to the land of certainty. All Great Ones show absolute detachment from objects of material existence, though They use them to run Their lives and help people.

The supreme reality of our Divinity is achieved by gradually discovering what is unreal, plane after plane, until we reach the Temple of the Divine Self. Those who discover the Divine Self become embodiments of certainty. Millions of people are drawn to them and see them as their hope, their path, their truth, their goal—their certainty.

People have a tendency to identify with or attach to objects that are not real. In attaching to such objects, they themselves lose their sense of reality. Physical plane objects at first are real for us, but when, through incarnation after incarnation, we experience their unreality, they become unreal for us. If we attach to the unreal after knowing it is so, we lose our path and our own life becomes unreal to us.

People without a sense of reality are a major source of pain and suffering in the world. They are those who butcher people to obtain their unreal goods and unreal life.

Chapter Eight

The Ageless Wisdom
And Religion

Great Individualities, age after age, saw what was real in the Universe and came to humanity and spoke about Their experiences, thoughts, and ideas which were later formulated as different religions, teachings, and disciplines.

Thus, the Ageless Wisdom is contained in the *Vedas, Upanishads, Vishnu Purana, Bhagavad Gita, Books of Moses, Kaballa, New Testament, Mahabharata, Koran, Yoga Sutras of Patanjali,* in Mithraism, Hinduism, Buddhism, Taoism, Zoroastrianism, Sufism, the teachings of the Mayans and Aztecs, the American Indians and the teachings of Shankaracharya, also the teaching given by a great leader in Japan by the name of Nichiren Daishonin—not to mention that which has been imparted by many other great philosophers, scientists, and artists throughout the world. This, in general, is the Wisdom given to humanity.

Throughout time Teachers appeared in many places in the world, revealing the Teaching in China, Egypt, Greece, England, Armenia, the Middle East, India, South America, Africa, and so on, organizing special schools which were founded in the spirit of the Ageless Wisdom.

In the Twentieth Century, in the vast ocean of generalized Teaching, specialized Teachings were given in various stages to certain Initiates by great Teachers. The most prominent and influential works in the specialized Teachings were given to three great persons:[1]

- H.P. Blavatsky

- Alice A. Bailey

- Helena Roerich

These Teachings are for serious students of Wisdom. These three remarkable women broke many crystallizations which were casting a shadow over the planet and the mind of humanity, and they gave their students a sense of true certainty. All three of them recognized the supreme beauty of Lord Buddha, Moses, Krishna, Christ, Mohammed, and all other Great Ones all over the world. They emphasized the reality of the Higher Worlds, the Brotherhood of man, and revealed a great vision for humanity. They especially emphasized spiritual discipline, striving, compassion, and cooperation among all the children of the Most High.

The general Teachings combined with these specialized Teachings which have been given to humanity are just parts of an iceberg, the body of which remains untouched in the depths of the ocean. No Teaching is absolute; no Teaching is complete. All are fragments. How can it be otherwise in view of Infinite Space— millions of light-years of depth existing in the stars, a grain of sand on the seashore, the infinitesimally small brain of the human being?

---

1. An interesting account of these three teachers is given in *Three Remarkable Women* by Harold Balyoz (Flagstaff, AZ: Altai Publishers, 1986).

One night my two-year-old son asked our neighbor and close friend, "How were the stars created?" The man answered, "One day God was playing with firecrackers and they exploded, sending the sparks all over the sky. That is what you see." "Now I understand," my son said. This is the current consciousness of humanity. How can God tell us about all that He created, about all that He is, when we are not even one month old compared to what He is? Yet some people act as if their teaching or religion were the whole picture—exactly like a person who loses his car, and then one day while walking through the desert finds the carburetor of a car and begins exclaiming, "I found a car! I now have a car!" But he can neither ride in that carburetor nor drive it. This is often how people act when they find a piece of the Ageless Wisdom: They think they have found all Wisdom, and they do not look any further to discover the other parts necessary to make that Wisdom relatively complete.

No Teaching can be absolute because of two factors: the one who gives and the one who receives. Both are pilgrims on the Path toward the Most High. How can they understand and formulate the Wisdom found in the Source of Light? The giver of the Teaching has relative knowledge compared to the Wisdom of that Source. Those who receive the Teaching are travelers on this dark and devastated planet.

The Teaching is imparted on a gradient scale. As the Teaching is actualized in the lives of the recipients, greater Teachers are sent to impart greater Teachings of Wisdom. The recipients are the decisive factor which determines how much Wisdom can be imparted by the Great Ones. If humanity remains at the kindergarten level and refuses to advance toward perfection, the Teachers at the university level will not be able to impart their Teaching.

Yet, masses of people proselytize that they have "the only way to fly." Those fanatics who make their religions "the only way to fly" are those who deliberately use fanaticism to reach certain separative goals, or psychologically they hide their uncertainty, trying to create a pseudo-certainty in the form of fanaticism.

One day it will be revealed that all fanatics who have destroyed people in the name of religion or beliefs were criminals before they began committing bigger crimes. A guilt complex covers itself in many ways, in many forms. But it cannot hide one thing: the nature of its violence, separatism, and hatred.

Closely observe those who profess that their beliefs are the only way to salvation, and you will find not only violence in their speech but also future plans to attack those who do not kneel before them. This is how people like Hitler come into being.

The unfortunate thing is that after a short while these hypocrites become associated with various departments of the Teaching and make the Teaching a marketplace for their own business and personal gain. Because of their self-interests, they refuse others and proclaim that only their teaching is correct, while all others are false. Unfortunately, this has even happened among the followers of recent great Teachers. Those who did not understand the Teaching began rejecting others and refusing to cooperate with each other. This happens in all sections of the Teaching because of ignorant and selfish people.

When the greater students of Wisdom achieve certain positions in the world, they will try to synthesize the Teaching given to humanity from the inception of time into the future. Only through synthesis will the Teaching be understood in its entire beauty. It is synthesis that will unite not only the parts of the Teaching but also all the followers of the Teaching. Thus, the Brotherhood of humanity will no longer be a dream; it will be a fact.

The Ageless Wisdom is a jewel, a precious stone from the Treasury of the Most High. This Treasury is unlimited, boundless, and infinite. Such an understanding makes us humble in the presence of the Most High.

Inclusiveness and discrimination are the greatest virtues of the soul. It is through inclusiveness and discrimination that the "little self" of man discovers the Cosmic Self. Inclusiveness is the urge to expand into the All-Self. Discrimination is the sense that saves time, suffering, pain, and failure on the Path.

Each expansion is a deeper penetration into the Treasure of the Most High.

Chapter Nine

Future Greatness

The Teaching of the Ageless Wisdom places a very strong emphasis on the existence of Higher Beings and on the group of Great Ones which is called the Hierarchy.

The Ageless Wisdom directs man's consciousness toward the future.

The concept of a Great One, a Master, the concepts of the Hierarchy and of the future go parallel in the pages of the Teaching.

In fact, the study about Masters, about the Hierarchy, is the study of the future.

A Master is not a dream, nor a thoughtform, nor a memory, nor a myth, but He is our future, as the oak tree is the future of an acorn.

When a person talks about Masters, some people feel uneasy because they think that Masters do not exist or Masters are those about whom some freaks talk.

But real Masters exist as, for example, a master mechanic exists; a master of space science exists; a master of mathematics exists; a master of arts exists; a master leader exists. Who are these masters? They are those who are relatively perfect in the field of their endeavor.

Masters are Those Who strive toward perfection and stand higher than those who are on the same path. Those who believe that they can endlessly improve and reach perfection are those who believe in Masters. One cannot advance if he does not believe that he can advance. . . and if one advances, eventually how much distance is there between him and those who never aspire to advance?

Every one of us must have a vision in his heart of a future mastery.

Each man eventually will achieve mastery over matter, time, and space and will be a Master.

A Master was a man who worked very hard, served sacrificially, and let his light shine out though his personality vehicles.

Life after life one masters not only his vehicles but also pays his karmic debts and purifies his life to such a degree that he no longer lives for himself but for life as a whole. As he goes beyond his little self, he radiates more joy, more bliss, and establishes closer and better relationships with all living forms.

The sense of immortality deepens in one's heart when he steps beyond his selfish interests. In thinking about the Master, the future, we liberate ourselves from our present limitations, release our mind from manifold traps, and stand in the light of the future.

The future is a vision. Once we build the vision of the future within us, we evoke energy from our Innermost Core. The vision acts as a transmitter of energy from higher sources.

The future is not only a vision but also it is a sphere of energy. When one thinks, talks, and writes about the future, he releases energy from his Innermost Core. Energy follows thought. The Core within our human form is our future, is the future. In thinking and talking about the future, we raise our consciousness to a higher level. As we raise our consciousness higher, we go closer to our true Self—to our future.

A man strives to be a personality, and eventually he integrates his physical, emotional, and mental nature and becomes a personality. The future of the personality is to become a living human soul. When a person aspires toward Soul consciousness, to the realms of the Soul, he eventually builds bridges between the personality and Soul. The bridge then brings personality and Soul closer to each other, until they form a fusion, which is called Soul-infusion.

When a man becomes a soul, he aspires toward the future, the Self—and again his aspiration, his thoughts, his meditations and striving build a bridge between the Soul awareness and the Self.

This awareness evokes energies from the Self which help to build the bridge or link between the human soul and the Self until they eventually become one.

Thus, through aspiring and striving toward the Self, you become the Self, you become the future which was waiting for you for ages.

Such a progressive development and unfoldment bring greater impressions and inspirations from your higher realms, vitalize your intellect, your mind, your brain, and polarize them toward the future.

As one polarizes toward the future, he becomes more radioactive, loving, energetic, creative, and beautiful. Nobility, solemnity, and grandeur radiate from him like the fragrances of rare flowers. Thus, one transforms his life by thinking about the future.

A Master is the symbol of the future of a man. The Hierarchy is the symbol of the future of humanity. When one thinks about the Masters or the Hierarchy, he projects electrical threads toward Them and establishes contacts with Great Ones.

Thinking is an activity to establish relationships. When you think about someone, your mind takes the thread of energy and ties you to the object. Thus, through thinking about someone, you tie yourself with him.

You can think about an object, even about stars, and you tie yourself to them, and the thread tying you turns into a thread of transmission of energy from the object.

In thinking about Great Ones, you establish a thread of contact with Them, and Their energy slowly finds the way through the thread to flow into your aura and, later, into your consciousness. That is why we are advised to hold in our heart the Hand of our Master.

The thread of communication between a man and the Master or Ashram or Hierarchy invites Their attention toward us.

Attention is a flow of energy. Through Their attention we receive energy, courage, fearlessness, joy, love, and vitality.

As the flow of energy from a Master to a disciple increases, the disciple advances on the Path toward his future.

As one advances toward the future, the Plan of the Hierarchy reveals itself to him, and the disciple dedicates all his life or many lives to serving the Plan.

When he advances more toward his future, the Purpose of the Great Life is revealed to him, and he dedicates his life in a great sacrificial service to orient humanity toward the realization of the Purpose.

Thinking about the Master and the Hierarchy eventually makes clear to you your present level, your present need, and reveals to you the existence of the endless Path of perfection. This realization exercises heavy pressure on you to strive toward the future and actualize your vision.

As one strives toward the future, he gains higher positions—leadership positions—in the world, and thus he shares his wisdom with humanity.

Spiritual position is not conditioned by diplomas and offices. It is a frequency through which you reach the hearts of millions and orient them toward beauty, goodness, and truth.

Masters belong to soul levels, or higher levels, and when a group thinks about, studies, and discusses Masters wisely, it evokes energy from Them, which integrates the group on soul or higher levels.

The souls of men are flames. The energy of the Masters touches those flames. As the flames grow and radiate, they draw each other into their field of influence and beauty.

This attraction appears in such a group as group integration, understanding, and fusion. As the fusion of the group increases, the group stands in front of the Hierarchy as a unit of service.

Only groups can transmit higher energies, energies which are able to change life and bring a new vision, vitality, and future.

Chapter Ten

Hierarchy And The Wisdom

One of the greatest treasures in the Treasury of the Most High is the Hierarchy. The Hierarchy is divided into seven major Ashrams, each having at its head a Great One Who synchronizes, synthesizes, and initiates new direction into the body of His Ashram.

Each Ashram is related to one of the seven fields of human endeavor. The seven Ashrams are related to the following:

- Politics
- Education
- Communication
- Arts
- Science
- Religion
- Economics and Finance

Each Ashram is trying to bestow certain "jewels of wisdom" in its particular field, urging those in that field to advance—not at the expense of others but for the benefit of each other—because the source of all their wisdom and knowledge is one—the Hierarchy.

This is why all fields of human endeavor advance only as fast as the personnel found in those fields can receive and assimilate the "treasures" being sent to them. There are found, however, unfortunate conditions in those who receive these treasures:

- vanity
- ego
- crystallization
- self-interest
- the spirit of separatism
- the spirit of exploitation
- the spirit of greed

So very often the treasures are squandered in the same way that a sudden large inheritance is misused. Some recipients of the treasures use this knowledge against human welfare by polluting, poisoning, and destroying Mother Nature, thereby causing great damage for coming generations. This is why we are told that knowledge will either destroy us or transform us.

Transformation becomes a fact only when people purify their motives, become inclusive, and work for the salvation of humanity and the lower kingdoms. No one can cross the river by destroying the bridge under his feet.

Those advanced human beings who are able to penetrate into the Ashram during sleep or through meditation can bring "treasures" down to Earth—especially if they are able to remember them. These people are the hope of the future. They can see the madness going on in all fields, and they try to warn humanity about the misuse of knowledge.

If humanity listens to them, then the planet will survive. If humanity ignores them and does not take the appropriate steps to stop the madness which is going on in science, technology, religion, politics, and so on, then humanity will destroy itself. Life will begin anew from an age of ashes—not even a stone age.

One of the greatest tragedies is that people are so preoccupied with their daily lives and so attached to their objects and possessions that they are cut from the supermundane worlds where the Ashrams exist. Imagine what a change we would witness if increasing numbers of people in all seven fields of human endeavor penetrated into the Ashrams and brought wisdom, knowledge, and direction to Earth every day.

Great Ones stress the importance of right meditation, again and again, because it is only through meditation that people will eventually be able to visit the Ashrams and bring back treasures for the transformation of life on Earth.

Chapter Eleven

The Principle And The Law
Of Hierarchy

The Principle of the Hierarchy is the principle of
the existence of inner Cores, around which run strivings, activities, and creativity. Everyone has a Core.
Every living form has a Core. Every organism and
organization has a Core, and it is this Core that
nourishes the cells, atoms, vehicles around the Core.

Such a principle does not conflict with the principle
of freedom, as people with their own free will achieve
positions suited to their level and consciousness.
Our consciousness can be within our Core or scattered
within the sphere of the Core. Whoever is in the Core,
worked for it; whoever is around the Core is there
because of his choice.

We must remember our consciousness cannot be in
the Core too long if it does not feed its spheres or the
co-workers around it and prepare them to be Cores.
There are also artificial cores which imitate that they
are Cores, but on the eternal Path, artificial cores fall
down and are thrown like wood from the ocean to the
shore.

Thus the Hierarchy has a Core which orchestrates
all creative activities in the Hierarchy. A nation has a
Core which is engaged in similar labor. This is also true
for a person whose Core orchestrates all his activities
as his consciousness expands and brings his vehicles
into closer contact with the Core.

The Law of the Hierarchy is the law of strict obser-
vance of the purpose and directives of the Core.

The Principle of the Hierarchy is the same principle
found in the human Core. This Principle has three
distinct characteristics:

1. Incessant striving toward perfection

2. Unfailing harmony with the direction of the
   Cosmic Heart

3. Absolute dedication to serve all that exists

These three characteristics of the Principle of the
Hierarchy are in every living unit. They must be
reached and activated if one wants to find the path
through the labyrinth of life.

The Law of the Hierarchy is the mode of reinforce-
ment of this principle upon those who are responding
to the principle.

The Law of the Hierarchy is divided into seven
branches, and may be formulated as follows:

1. The Law of Right Relationship

2. The Law of Unity and Synthesis

3. The Law of Attraction

4. The Law of Economy

5. The Law of Resurrection

6. The Law of Balance and Equilibrium

7. The Law of Sacrifice

Obedience to these seven laws leads the disciple to the
Principle of the Hierarchy.

The Law of Right Relationship is a law which must be observed from the moment one reaches the stage of being a conscious entity, and it must be observed into Infinity. Building right relationship is the only way that one can find his true path of progress in the existence as a whole. Right relationship is a creative response to all conscious actions going on in Cosmos.

No one can advance by disobeying the **Law of Unity and Synthesis.** Synthesis is right relationship between units. It is the law that opens the path of infinite expansion and cooperation with all that exists.

The Law of Attraction is the sensitivity to respond to the pull of the Cosmic Magnet and use the energies and forces available to lead the spark of light to the Central Core.

The Law of Economy is the right use of energy, force, matter, and space. It is the right use of thoughts, words, actions; the right use of incoming impressions, inspirations, and direction.

Right use means to use in accordance with the Plan of the Hierarchy and in harmony with the Divine Purpose—or in harmony with the conscience and responsibility.

The Law of Resurrection on higher planes is the law which helps us transcend our limitations and barriers and pass into more expanding horizons and into more glorious vehicles and relationships.

The Law of Balance and Equilibrium is used to make us masters or conquerors in agitated conditions, which can occur on any plane of Divine Existence. It enables us to go forward by surfing on the waves.

The Law of Sacrifice enables the advancing units to manifest the essential Divinity within.

Each true sacrifice is a spark of divine force given to the world to kindle the souls, to purify the world, and to pave the way toward greater and greater glories of achievement.

These seven laws are the formulation of the Principle of the Hierarchy.

Disciples and Initiates are under these laws, and transgression of these laws can have grave influences or effects in their life relationships and responsibilities.

The Hierarchy must be taken as the brotherhood of all those advanced human beings who, after conquering death, stay on the planet to help humanity continue its evolution in the best way possible and without losing too much time. Because of Their high achievement, we are told that They can watch the life of any disciple They want to see if he is making good progress, and occasionally They strengthen him on the Path. Thus, every disciple actually lives under Their watchful eyes.

One needs to be alert every minute and live according to the Principle and the Law of the Hierarchy.

> *Certainly the power of Hierarchy is the most vital, and only by this bridge can one build. Thus in the foundation of each great beginning is inlaid the energy imbued by the law of Hierarchy. Only upon the law of closest coalescence can one build. Only upon the basis of the affirmation of the principle of Hierarchy can one affirm the highest possibility. The creative will proclaims that a blended consciousness gives the decision of concordance.*[1]

---

1. Agni Yoga Society, *Hierarchy* (New York: Agni Yoga Society, 1977), para. 48.

There is a law in the universe according to which every living form strives to advance, to progress, to improve, and to perfect itself.

The Hierarchy is built when the links of those advanced forms found on different levels form a chain. Each link on the chain advances. Each chain is a station and also a living form.

To advance means to release concealed potentials within properly constructed vehicles.

To progress means to exercise influence on the advancing life-units within the environment, helping them to advance.

To improve means to have a better adjustment and integration with the environment and make the environment live in harmony with the challenge of advanced life-units.

To perfect is a process in which life-units follow the direction of the rhythm of the Cosmic Magnet.

Hence the Law of Hierarchy is a law challenging every life-unit to expand its consciousness-awareness and to gear itself with the direction of the Cosmic Magnet.

The Law of Hierarchy is the magnetic power of the Cosmic Magnet to make all life-units a part of the symphony of the Cosmic Magnet.

No constructive action is possible without the Law of Hierarchy.

Happiness, joy, freedom, and bliss are experienced only through advancement, progress, improvement, and perfection by the Law and in the Law of Hierarchy.

It is in this Law that awareness of continuity is actualized. It is in this Law that the importance of the Teacher is realized. It is in this Law that the life-unit realizes the utmost importance of striving and of self-generated efforts.

It is in this Law that the power of the sense of responsibility unfolds and leads the life-units to the awareness of the One Cosmic Self.

The beginning of every project, every plan, that will bring happiness, health, prosperity, and enlightenment is based on the Law of Hierarchy. All expansion on the path of Beauty, Goodness, Righteousness, Joy, and Freedom is based in the power of the Law of Hierarchy.

One of the major effects of this Law is the creation of the phenomena of cooperation. Cooperation is the builder. A sense of responsibility, cooperation, and gratitude are those powerful energies put in action by the Law of Hierarchy.

Gratitude conditions the life-units to absorb the possibilities, the blessings provided by the Law of Hierarchy.

The precious seed of spirit awakens to the vision of its Cosmic destiny when for the first time it registers the existence of the Law of Hierarchy.

When a reference is made about links and chains, people naturally think about their rings and the chains they hang around their neck. This is a useful technique of association. But links must be interpreted as bridges, as the antahkarana, as planes of existences, as spheres of communications, as units of consciousness in relation with "above and below," as sensitivity, as coordinating, relating, and fusing factors.

Chains can be interpreted as groups of advancing life-units, highly cooperative and interrelated; also, as power tools to make possible things that seem impossible.

A chain is also the symbol of a frequency. There are as many chains as atoms, but there is only one Law of Hierarchy which orchestrates each unit to aspire to the glory of the Cosmic Magnet.

Chapter Twelve

The Work Of Great Teachers

Every human being will one day become a great Teacher, a great person. No matter how many obstacles or hindrances we have, that urge to be perfect, beautiful, healthy, and prosperous is within us. It takes many ages before that urge awakens, but once it is awakened, nothing can stop our progress. A great fundamental statement is that the human being is destined to be great, to be the master of his life. To do so, he must conquer hindrances and obstacles inherited from the past, hindrances that exist in his environment, and hindrances collected in the subconscious.

I once visited a graveyard. Out of a crack in a marble tombstone grew a little tree, maybe fifteen inches tall. At that moment I realized that Nature instills energy and power in every seed to overcome any obstacle. Human beings are seeds, special seeds. That is why we have survived for so long and why we will survive for Eternity.

When we describe Great Ones, we create an inspiration which awakens the seed within us to become a Great One—not out of vanity or for the exploitation of others, but by virtue of our essence and destiny.

A Great One is a man or woman Who is able to destroy all those causes in the physical, emotional, and mental nature which will produce pain, suffering, and failure in the future. When a person begins to conquer the negative causes planted within himself, causes that will create future unhappiness, pain, and suffering in his life, he is becoming a Master.

It is so logical and clear. We have many blind urges and drives which we have collected throughout the ages. Our parents supplied us with many; our environment contributed as well; and we produced them with our own hallucinations, imagination, and wrong living.

A person spins himself a cocoon and buries himself in his own obstacles. He needs to find a way out of that cocoon and escape. He needs to pierce it and find a way to soar as a butterfly; he must have wings. It is not bad that he buries himself—if he is developing the possibility of having wings.

When a person feels that he has wings and escapes from his prison, he emerges into the open space of greatness. Greatness comes through obedience to the law that states, "Whatever you sow, you reap." Nature does not provide those things for which a person is not worthy. We must take the Kingdom of Heaven "by violence," which means heavy labor that refuses all of the unsound, insane things existing within us. Such are Masters.

We are on the path of mastery, but people do not believe this because they are hypnotized by their own failures, by the opinions of others, by their traditions and history. They cannot overcome this hypnotized state of mind which suggests that they are worth nothing, that they are powerless, senseless vegetables which will eventually disappear.

When you think about greatness, you grow. I read a story about the first man to climb Mount Everest. When he was asked why he wanted to climb it, he replied, "Because it is there!" Find the summit within yourself and say, "I am going to climb that mountain because the summit is challenging me." That challenge must be faced rigorously by conquering yourself, your false self, your false image, and by powerfully destroying your hypocrisy, lies, and irritations. Destroy these and you will find a way of escape; you will discover that you have developed two wings that are balanced and directed toward open space.

Great Teachers, Great Ones, never force Their Teaching as if it were absolute. Such action is a curse, a slander against God. No one is capable of knowing everything nor of saying what he believes is the absolute. Wars and bloodshed originate from this mistake. Great Ones know that Their Teaching, Their mind, Their power, is limited to a specific stage of perfection or evolution. For a Great One there is no "only way to fly."

A Great One knows that He is not absolute. He knows that whatever He is talking about is not absolute. He also knows that the people who listen to Him are in various stages of development, that they are not absolute and cannot understand absoluteness. By speaking in absolutes, people err, create dogmas, doctrines, and thus lead humanity to insanity. A great mistake is made when a person states, "A spirit told me. God recommended it." One must question who this person is to come in contact with the Highest and give His message to humanity? These are examples of illusion and vanity.

Great Ones never do this. They know Their limitations and the limitations of those who listen to Them. A Great One looks toward the sky, toward the stars, and thinks, "We are just one mile closer to Them." This is the true meaning of humility. Ignorant, vain, and stupid people "know" everything. Wise people and sages say that they know nothing. Socrates was once asked, "What do you know?" He replied, "I know one thing—that I do not know." Such is a Great One.

If you see signs of smallness, be careful. Fanaticism and absoluteness are signs of smallness. Great Ones never force Their Teaching on the consciousness of humanity or attract people with fear, bribery, or advertisements. Did you ever see a Master advertise Himself? Pseudo-masters do this; Great Ones never do.

The enemies of greatness create subtle obstacles. They look at artificial pearls and say, "How beautiful!" so that we will buy them and not search for real pearls. They pollute our vision. But Great Ones never teach with threats or bribery. Some people insist, "You will go to hell, you sinners, if you do not attend our church and pay a certain huge sum of money. God will abandon you, and then what will happen? You will be destroyed, annihilated." They threaten us in the name of our future greatness. But if God is within us, why would He do such things?

Any time you sense a threat, use caution. Deception and fear lurk behind threats. People have created so much falsehood. Everywhere you turn, there are obstacles to overcome. But the human spirit will eventually succeed, if striving exists.

Fear creates antagonism. Fear creates hypocrisy. Fear creates imitation. Fear herds "cattle" around you who pretend that they are worshiping, striving people—and you become buried by these cattle, like a cowboy in a stampede.

Unfortunately, the leaders of humanity—deplorably, painfully, and insufferably—use fear techniques. They destroy the national and international health, freedom, blooming, expansion, and radioactivity of the human soul by using fear techniques.

Insurance companies know all about using fear. Three days after my arrival in the United States, a tall man came to my home and knocked on the door. Because of the way he was dressed and the way he stood, I thought he must be somebody important, so I opened the door to speak with him. He told me he was an insurance salesman and said, "Do you know what will happen to you if you become sick?" "I am not going to be sick," I said. "Well," he said, "this is the United States." "My gosh," I said, "where have I come? What will happen?" He said, "Oh, they will come and take your house, your furniture—everything." I asked him how I could prevent that. "Well," he said, "sign this." I did not know anything about insurance, but I told him to get lost. He left and never returned. From that moment on there was a great wound in me. Why do people want to exploit others through fear and threats?

A man once came to me for counseling who said, "I cannot handle my wife." "Okay," I said, "bring her with you and let's talk together." The next session I observed that every time he opened his mouth, he threatened her. He would say, "I will divorce you; I will take you to court and not support you. I will beat you." I finally asked him to stop. Everything became clear.

Right human relations and greatness cannot bloom in any person if fear techniques are used. Nations are destroyed when their rulers make the people of the nation live in fear. Great Teachers never do this. In looking through history to see why nations disappeared, you will find a common factor: fear dominated their lives.

A family is successful, beautiful, and prosperous if there is no fear. Once fear starts in a family, the children will do the most offensive things behind their parents' backs. The family will disintegrate and lose its prosperity and joy if it lives in fear. Fear creates hypocritical and antagonistic people.

Great Ones labor to erase fear and help humanity bloom. They demonstrate intense labor. Laziness does not exist in Them. This is because They are *sattvic,* which means They have a rhythmic spirit and manifest tireless labor. There is no laziness or inertia in Them; every minute, every day, They do something to help others, to help Themselves, to help God. God needs more helpers than we do!

It is through labor that the diamond in you will be polished. That diamond is the real you, and it must be polished through incessant labor—physical, emotional, mental, spiritual, and group labor. A person cannot be lazy if he has a dream of greatness because the peak of the mountain is perceived. He will climb through dark, dangerous, and winding roads. . . because the summit is there.

Great Ones do not count the days, months, hours, years. . . or even lives. Time does not exist for Them. Only Eternity and the goal exist.

One day I attended a lecture on the subject of the Great Ones. The speaker began describing Them by saying, "Great Ones are Those Who have long beards and lots of money. They have the power to kill and to raid." I decided I had better leave. Great Ones are sometimes presented to us with distorted images so that we come to hate Them. Intelligent people are able to see the motivation behind the distortion created by crazy people.

Great Ones are executives of the major departments of Nature. Their greatness is only proved by the deeds They leave behind.

Greatness is the ability to work and labor to reach your purpose without feeling tired. There is a secret in Nature: Man is a generator of energy which functions only if he strives toward greatness and encourages others to strive toward greatness. If a person does not strive toward greatness, this generator does not function.

Try striving and see how your energy increases. Make others great or try to make them great. We are bombarded by hypnotic suggestions which tell us, "Think only of yourself; to hell with the others. Exploit them, step on them, beat them down." This is a false philosophy.

The Ageless Wisdom states that a person never advances unless he makes others advance; he will never become really prosperous and enjoy life unless he makes others prosperous and able to enjoy their lives. We are flooded by false philosophies. Destroy them and begin opening yourself to a new consciousness, one which believes that you exist only if you make other people exist. This is the supreme philosophy. But contemporary philosophy states that we exist only by destroying others. We have tried this for the last eighteen million years, and it has not worked yet because it is false.

Create friends; make them exist so that all of us exist. We are just like thousands of electric light bulbs through which One Electricity flows. For the sake of the One Electricity, we must make each other exist so that more light shines out. If you destroy this bulb, and then that one, and then another one, leaving only your own bulb, there is so little light that you live in darkness. Increase the number of bulbs, make them healthy and prosperous, and you will become great because you are in greatness, in God.

Position and recognition do not affect a Great One. Pseudo-leaders crave recognition. They wonder if they are going to get a promotion. Such a person has no foundation. Real greatness is indifferent to whether people recognize you or not, whether you are abandoned or not, whether you receive a position or not. A Great one has position because He is Himself. He does not depend on outside conditions.

If we want to be Great Ones, we need to exercise these rules and regulations, laws and principles, or else we will remain the same idiots that we were in the past. There is a path of greatness; there is a path of degeneration. We need to choose which one to follow. The possibility of greatness is always with us. We need to turn on the switches of the generator by working for the greatness of others. Have an attitude which says, "Do not worry about me; I only want your happiness. Do not worry about my business; I only want to put you in the right direction so that you will become rich. Do not worry about my sleep; I want you to have the proper rest." Through this kind of attitude, greatness awakens.

Great Ones are not trapped by the false images others create about Them. In discussing greatness, a man once told me that he wanted to be a king—as if being a king were greatness. "If I am a king, I can go anywhere any time I want and conquer people," he said. This is not greatness. The violation of the rights of other people is a sign of smallness. The violation of the rights of people to exist, to be happy, prosperous, and successful is the greatest violation against our own survival.

A person must come to realize that a Great One exists within himself. By actualizing his own greatness, he sees that he has found a Great Teacher, one that cannot be missed. If I say that a Great Teacher is in the Himalayas, that He is sitting in the vortices or in a cave, people will search for Eternity and never find Him. Only greatness finds greatness.

Security is found only in self-actualization. There is no real security in the world. People created the word "security"; but such a condition does not exist. We think it exists, we hope it exists, and we create empires trying to establish security. But where is security when one little earthquake can take all of us? How do we know that this will not happen?

There is no security in this sense. A man who showed me his muscles one day called me five days later to tell me he had AIDS. Real security is achieved only by unveiling our Divinity so that we are no longer conditioned by those things which we once believed created security. Nothing and no one can create security until the Fire within starts to bloom and unveil Itself. This makes a person secure for Eternity.

"Secure" people were flying in a jet one day; two hundred and eighty people were killed when that plane crashed. Security is the effort to make Divinity exist, bloom, and express Itself. This is the diamond that you will never lose.

A country was once attacked by another. A soldier, armed with a dagger, approached a person who was working on a mathematical problem. The man said to the soldier, "Please let me have two or three more minutes until I solve this problem." The soldier replied,

"No, you are the enemy," and stabbed him in the back. Before the person died he said, "You can take my life, but not my mind." Such beingness is a state of security.

Do you have something secure to carry with you besides your "trash bags"? Try to know, to do, to serve. But above all, try to be. Our true beingness is the source of all creative labor.

Every one of us is going to become a Great One, as long as each one of us strives to be perfect and helps others be perfect—no matter what failures, hindrances, and obstacles we meet on the Path.

Greatness is achieved not by knowing but by being great.

Chapter Thirteen

Distortion

It is very important not to read any book about the Ageless Wisdom which is prostituted for the purpose of separatism, racism, the political or economic gain of one group over another, or for the purpose of emphasizing a particular nation or race at the expense of another.

Distortion of the Ageless Wisdom is widespread. People often use the Ageless Wisdom to exploit others or to draw attention to their national or racial interests. People distort the Ageless Wisdom to cover up their own ugliness and to feed their pride and vanity.

They distort the Ageless Wisdom through channeling, mediumistic practices, statements and instructions, through lower psychic phenomena, magic, witchcraft, hypnotism, and so on. Each distortion has a purpose—a selfish, separative, and ugly purpose. We are told that the karma of distorters is very heavy.

There are, of course, conscious and unconscious distorters. Conscious distorters use every kind of forgery to change the Teaching to confuse people. These distorters are called hypocrites, and Christ warned His disciples to stay away from such people.

How can we discriminate between a distortion and something which is revealed and given to us as an addition to the Teaching? A new facet of the Teaching adds to the construction of the Teaching. It is in harmony with the Teaching and further reveals the greater beauties hidden in the Teaching. New revelations never contradict older ones but bring greater light to the older revelations.

New revelations are not founded on sectarianism, racism, or separative interests. They are not given in the heat of emotion and evangelism. New and higher parts of the Teaching do not make claims, show off, or demonstrate competitiveness. They make the Teaching more complete and fill a deeper need of the people without destroying anything in those people. They radiate solemnity, purity, and beauty.

On the other hand, false or falsified teachings are full of claims of infallibility and demand attention. They are separative, aggressive, pompous, noisy, and used for selfish political or economic ends and serve only self interest.

Chapter Fourteen

Joy In The Teaching

In the *Lotus Sutra*, Gautama Buddha makes a very important statement in describing future advanced human beings:

Born purely,
through the method of transformation,
they will adorn their bodies with perfect marks.
Their food will be only
the joy of meditation and
the joy of the Teaching.
And they will never think to nourish themselves
with any other kind of food.[1]

What is the joy of the Teaching? It is the joy that pure wisdom—the Truth—gives to a person. The Teaching—which reveals the depths of existence, the laws ruling existence, the path of transcendence, and the Core of the Universe which expands our consciousness and develops our higher senses to contact higher realities—is the source of joy. Joy is an energy which is assimilated by our higher centers and distributed to our vehicles as food and nourishment.

We are told that joy is the food of Angels. We can increasingly partake of this nourishment as we drop our self-interest, ego, vanity, and separatism. Joyful

---

1. Compiled by author.

people eat less food and labor longer. Joyless people continuously eat but feel hungry and weak.

We tested this once in the monastery. The governing board of the monastery divided the student body into two groups. Then it created joyful events for thirty-six hours for one group. Those in the first group had no time to eat; they enjoyed the dancing, comedies, songs, and games the entire time. The other group was shown sad and violent movies and dramas, and they were told sad stories. Many of these students could not stay longer than five hours, and most of them went to their rooms in sadness.

During the days that followed, those who had joyful experiences slept very deeply and very well. They were very positive in their attitudes and were deeply joyful upon resuming their daily routine. However, those who had been subjected to the negative influence of the sad and violent movies and stories were like beaten dogs—negative, nervous, and irritable. Such experiments could be conducted in a more scientific way to find out how and why joy nourishes the nervous system.

The Teaching is a flow of joy. The Teaching comes from Higher Spheres, bringing rare and glorified substance from those spheres which literally fill the "batteries" of people—their nervous system, their muscles and bloodstream, and so on. We must accustom ourselves to thinking that joy is a substance, like a ray of light, and that it is the most valuable healing substance in existence. This is why Christ said, "The words which I have spoken to you are spirit, and life."[2] Charged with the joy of the Teaching, people become invincible and

---

2. John 6:63

immune to any dark attack. They can carry out their labor of love, even unto death.

The second food for advanced human beings is the joy of meditation. No one can understand this unless he experiences the deepening joy which comes from persistent meditation, carried out even under the most trying conditions. The joy that comes from meditation is a nourishing, healing, and uplifting substance which is drawn from Higher Spheres through contact by means of meditation.

In real meditation, one slowly detaches himself from his body and physical concerns, from his emotional nature and problems, from his mental nature and worries, anxieties, problems, subconscious currents, and hypnotic suggestions—like an airplane which gradually rises above the pollution and disturbances found in the lower atmosphere and penetrates into the light above the clouds of daily life.

The joy of meditation starts when the consciousness begins to open itself to the light of new inspirations, impressions, ideas, visions, and revelations, each being substantial food not only for the soul but for all vehicles. This is the meaning of what Christ said in the wilderness while He was fasting for forty days: "Not by bread alone that man can live, but by every word which comes from the mouth of God."[3]

"Every word" is the realm of light, the realm of pure Wisdom and the pure Teaching, the sphere of law and knowledge into which the one who meditates penetrates. As a person gradually penetrates into the realm of pure ideas, he charges his whole being with

---

3. Matthew 4:4

these ideas, which carry with them the joy of the Higher Spheres, awakening in him the sleeping lion.

There are many kinds of joy that great Teachers of humanity emphasize. For example, in another section of the *Lotus Sutra* Lord Buddha says,

> *When people hear that they shall attain Bud-dhahood, these people are filled with a great joy which permeates their bodies.*

Christ said,

> *I have spoken these things to you, that my joy may be in you, and that your joy may be full.*[4]

> *So you also are depressed; but I will see you again, and your heart will rejoice, and your joy no man will take away from you.*[5]

In the *Upanishads* we read:

> *A man becomes like an ocean when he sees unity in all Creation. This is the highest achieve-ment. This is the highest sphere a man can achieve. This is the highest joy and bliss. Other creatures live only from such a bliss.*[6]

---

4. John 15:11
5. John 16:22
6. *Brihad Aranyaka Upanishad,* Verse 31, author's trans.

Whenever words fail,
whenever the mind fails in the path
of its attainment,
it is enough for him
to have the bliss of Brahma,
by which all his fears
are dispersed. [7]

For who indeed will breathe,
who would live,
if there were not this bliss
in Space! [8]

In the *Upanishads*, the highest vehicle of the Self is called the body of bliss.

There is a joy which is evoked through sacrificial service and heroic labor. No joy can surpass the joy that one feels when he sacrifices his life for the redemption and transformation of humanity. Every act of sacrificial service to anyone in the world opens within us the currents of the energy of joy, which charges our soul and body and regenerates our whole system.

We will save much time, money, and energy; we will save on doctor and hospital bills and avoid much suffering and pain only if we work hard to release the rivers of joy within and live, move, and have our being in joy.

---

7. *Taittiriya Upanishad,* Fourth Anuvaka.

8. *Ibid.,* Seventh Anuvaka.

Joy is the feeling that one is dedicated to a great cause, accepting the suffering that is inseparable from such dedication.

M.M. says,

> *Only in the acceptance of suffering is born the embryo of the joy of wisdom. It cannot be achieved without suffering. Only with Us is this joy born.*[9]

Dedication is a very healing factor. The greater a person's dedication, the greater is the resultant integrity in the human psyche. It is possible to cure many psychic disturbances in people by teaching them the way of dedication and by challenging them to dedicate all that is possible to a great cause.

Once dedication becomes a fact in one's life, the acceptance of suffering for a great cause is simply welcomed in the heart. It is at this moment that joy spreads and gradually fills the whole life of the dedicated person.

Every sincere dedication to the Common Good eventually brings a person into contact with the Great Ones. It is this contact that makes the flame of joy permanent and clear.

People are sometimes born with such a flame. They intuitively know the direction they will take and every suffering in their life is accepted as the act of the flame.

On the path of dedication, suffering makes a person more useful, while joy helps him spread his wisdom

---

9. Agni Yoga Society, *Supermundane.*

more realistically. For a dedicated person, joy is a great magnet which draws to him co-workers in whom the flame of joy is blooming.

For a dedicated person, joy is a line of contact with Those Who watch the steps of Their co-workers and continuously send Wisdom to feed the souls of the dedicated ones.

In every life, joy increases through suffering and dedication, as the steps of the pilgrim approach the borders of the Great Ones.

Chapter Fifteen

Slandering The Teaching

The Teaching is the Ageless Wisdom. All laws, principles and revelations imparted to humanity in the past, present, and future are from the Teaching. The Teaching is recognized by seven signs which proclaim the following principles:

1. The essential Divinity of every living being

2. The oneness of the imminent and transcendent Divinity in man and in the Universe

3. The path of Beauty, Goodness, Righteousness, Joy, and Freedom as a link between the imminent and transcendent natures of Divinity

4. The Law of Cause and Effect and the Law of Reincarnation

5. The nine states of consciousness and the nine states of initiation toward liberation and infinite attainment

6. The Law of Extinction

7. The Law of Sacrifice and Compassion

These are the seven wheels of Wisdom, the seven drums of the Teaching, the seven trumpets of the seven Archangels.

All of this Wisdom has been given to humanity on various levels, in various ways, and through various symbols from the dawn of life on this planet. The Teaching is given to every nation, and it is received in accordance with the nation's level and labor.

The Teaching has no past, present, or future. These conditions are the reactions and responses of our consciousness. If our consciousness is fully awake, the Teaching is perceived in the eternal now. The karma of a nation or an individual is the result of reaction to the Teaching.

Those who have been devoted and earnestly dedicated to the Teaching in the past, in the present, and who will do so in the future are those who are called aspirants, disciples, Initiates, Arhats, Masters, Chohans, and Resurrected Ones—or Those Who entered into the "extinction" of the seeds of karma.

Any form of slander against the Teaching has fatal consequences in the destiny of a person. Forms of slander in our thoughts, words, and emotional reactions and responses can be formulated as follows:

1. Indifference to the Teaching

2. Violation of the principles of the Teaching

3. Intentional distortion of the principles of the Teaching

4. Organized crimes, terrorism, war and revolution to prevent unity and freedom, while establishing totalitarianism and spreading corruption

5. Use of the Teaching to increase personal income, vanity, influence, and exploitation of people

6. Organized activities which do the following:

   a. prevent the propagation of the Teaching

   b. hurt, kill, or destroy the servants of the Teaching and their groups or organizations and create endless difficulties which prevent their successors from rendering service

   c. curse, mock, or ridicule the Teaching and objects of worship of the Teaching

   d. accept the Teaching, but still do the following:

      1) live a life contrary to the Teaching

      2) have time and opportunity for the Teaching but instead become caught in inertia and laziness, failing to practice it

      3) distract the attention of the devotees of the Teaching, leading them to pleasures or to involvement in time-and-energy-consuming projects and activities which are opposed to the principles of the Teaching

      4) fail to recognize the true leaders of the Teaching, or ignore them because of jealousy and self-interest, because

of their different approaches, schools
or interpretations of the seven principles

5) talk, write, or think in ways which

— are against the Hierarchy, or
against those who brought the
principles of right human relations, beauty, light, true leadership, and wisdom to humanity

— are against those who have
sacrificed themselves to unite,
cooperate, and fulfill the principle of unity

— create barriers or traps for
those who try to walk the Path
projected by the Teaching

— create antagonism and
animosity among those groups
which try to propagate the
Teaching in different ter-
minologies, on different levels,
and in relation to their understanding and needs

Individuals, groups, and nations can slander the
Teaching in all seven fields of human endeavor by
working against the seven principles of the Teaching.
The Teaching is actually the foundation of life—and is
life itself. Without the Teaching, life could not proceed
to its destination and reveal its potentials and possibilities.

The Teaching runs through all phases and forms of life, just as electricity flows through a network of wires. It is the greatest crime to hinder the flow of the Teaching or to act against it. We humans think that the Teaching is given only for humanity, but this is not true. Each kingdom of nature has its own Teaching, its own head Teachers. All kingdoms by various means and expedient devices are led on the Path of progress and perfection. The Teaching is the Life Thread of all living forms. Any attack or slander against the Teaching is the greatest crime against life itself.

If you want to know why certain people, groups and nations failed and were destroyed or were successful and flourished in the past, study their relationship to the Teaching. If you want to know the future of individuals, groups, and nations, study their present life in relation to the Teaching and you will be able clearly to forecast their future.

The future for individuals is approximately from seventy years of life to many future lives. The future for a group is from fifty to three hundred years or future group-incarnations. The future for a nation (political entity) is four hundred and ninety years— under one form of constitution, ruler, or form of government.

Nations do not incarnate in the same way that humans do. The individuals of different nationalities are attracted to certain nations either by their hatred and karmic debts or through their admiration and love.

The intelligent student of history will be able to see the exact causes of events which have occurred in a national Life Thread. Events have a variety of causes which in turn have various results:

1. Slander of the Teaching by a certain percentage of the people

2. Indifference toward the Teaching

3. Persecution of great Teachers

4. Reverence to the Teaching and the Teachers

5. Full-hearted assistance given to the principles of the Teaching

Students of history can discover exactly when and where the leaders of certain nations failed to respect the Teaching or succeeded in honoring the Teaching. The phases through which a nation passes reflect its relation to the Teaching.

It is true that those individuals who live and move and have their being in the principles of the Teaching will reach a stage of unfoldment called "Buddhahood" or "Christ-consciousness" where their Inner Divinity will shine out and create a life of Beauty, Goodness, Righteousness, Joy, and Freedom.

But those who live against the principles of the Teaching will find their Inner Divinity extinguished, creating for themselves an environment and a life of

- darkness
- crime
- anti-survival modes of living
- ugliness
- violence
- corruption
- disease
- degeneration

Life is an Entity; all the manifested forms of life are expressions of that Entity. When one lives within the principles of the Teaching, he will not only intuitively grasp the Purpose of that Entity and cooperate with it, but he will also synchronize his expressed forms of activity on the mental, emotional, and physical planes with the direction of that greater Purpose.

Thus, individuals, groups, or nations will put themselves in gear with that supreme and almighty Entity of Life, with Its Purpose, and turn into a current of energy running toward the beauty of Infinity.

Chapter Sixteen

Approach To The Teaching

People approach the Teaching as if it were a supermarket from which they can buy all that they need for their stomachs and bodies. But the Teaching is given to cause radioactivity and decentralization of self-interest and to make people learn the science of sacrificial service.

As long as one approaches the Teaching as if it were a supermarket, he will not profit spiritually from it, although he can use whatever he collects from the supermarket to entertain himself and others and thus waste the treasury of the Teaching. Wasting the Teaching can produce sad consequences due to the following reasons:

a. You lose your magnetism.

b. You turn into a hypocrite.

c. You exploit people for your own pleasure.

d. You blind your inner eye and inner ear.

e. You accumulate heavy karma.

f. You fall into isolation.

g. You are born into unfortunate circumstances in your next incarnation.

Just as people like to collect items of interest for their home, they also tend to collect ideas and information from the Teaching to be added to their mental collections, whereas the Teaching is only to be used for the actualization of their higher potentials and to cause transformation in their life.

The Teaching must be approached also with the intent to learn the following:

- How to love

- How to lose self-interest

- How to serve

- How to increase joy and freedom

- How to liberate people

The Teaching invites us not only to know but also to be. The road leading to beingness must be penetrated. In the Teaching of the Lord Buddha, the Enlightened One, five levels of penetration are given. These stand before us as a challenge, as a vision for all who want to tread the Path.

1. Divine Eye—clear seeing

2. Divine Ear—clear hearing

3. Knowledge of the thoughts of others

4. Recollection of former incarnations

5. Deeds leading to magical powers and release

The Divine Eye comes into being when a person lives, acts, speaks, and thinks in the light.

The Divine Ear comes into being when one purifies and frees his whole nature from egotism, vanity, and separatism.

Knowledge of the thoughts of others is achieved when the person's heart is totally purified.

Recollection of former incarnations is achieved when one penetrates into the treasury of the Chalice at the time of absolute renunciation.

Magical powers are achieved when one loses himself in the One Self.

The Teaching is not a supermarket but a center for transfiguration and mastery. As yet, most of the places of worship are not centers where people can learn how to renounce their glamors, illusions, maya, ego, and vanity, or learn how to step on the not-self. They are not yet centers where people enter the path of discipleship. Places of worship are usually places of emotional entertainment and abodes of personal "security." Some of them are mainly occupied with easing the path of glamor for others or occupied with taking advantage of others through psychic glamors and manipulative techniques. Many still refuse those people who point out their wounds and mistakes; they are still absorbed in the material world for most of their life.

It seems very strange that most people use the Teaching like some sort of personal medication. They "take" the Teaching because, after they hear uplifting lectures and read a spiritual book or two or have a good meditation, they experience the following:

- They feel very good.
- They enjoy life more.
- Their house is in better shape.
- They can make more money.
- Their family loves them more.

These results are good, but the goals of the Teaching extend beyond a person's personal pleasures and comforts, beyond his business and his home. We seldom hear people telling us that they love the Teaching because of any of the following reasons:

1. Their field of service to others improves.

2. Their viewpoints change.

3. Larger fields of labor open to them, and they have become extremely busy serving in them.

4. They experience self-forgetfulness and have begun to understand the meaning of self sacrifice.

5. They see greater light in people and see the efforts that others are making to make this world a better place.

6. They are taking many risks to be of service to the Teaching.

7. They are realizing their weaknesses and glamors and see how these prevent them from becoming a better servant to humanity.

These seven points signal a sincere approach to the Teaching, indicating that a person is beginning to understand the Teaching. It is important to serve the Teaching instead of making the Teaching serve us.

People study the Teaching for three main reasons. The first reason is to gain benefit, good health, good business, good relationships with people, good feelings, calmness, creative ideas and thoughts. Such people use the Teaching to improve their own lives and make themselves rich and feel that they are safe and secure.

The second reason is to help other individuals, groups, nations, and humanity; to teach others the path of health, happiness, prosperity, and peace; to study and apply the Teaching to lead human evolution forward and bring universal transformation, making transformation reach such a degree that humanity finds ways to communicate consciously with the Higher Worlds.

Others study the Teaching to insult and slander the Teaching and Teachers, to distort principles, and to present the Teaching to the public in such a way that they evoke rejection and even ridicule. The people in this third category use every available device of intellect to find ways and means to defile the Teaching. Sometimes they masquerade as knowing the Teachings of Great Ones and with subtle hints sow the seeds of doubt and slander.

There are specialized groups which study the various ways and means to attack with great power the Teachings and the Teachers. It is in these groups that the origin of distortion lies. People begin to believe that the Teaching is really dangerous and harmful. This happens when people do not have access to the right Teaching, and they base their conclusions on the writings and speeches of those who are consciously engaged in distorting the Teaching.

What is the future of these three categories?

In passing through various psychological crises, the first group of people, those who study to gain benefit, will eventually make a breakthrough and graduate to the second group where, through a developing and expanding consciousness, they will handle the Teaching for the good of all.

It sometimes happens, however, that their egos become so nourished by the Teaching that they turn into fanatics or sectarians and form a separative teaching by themselves with what little they know. Such people complicate and disturb their brains to such a degree that they eventually fall into the third category and become enemies of the Teaching.

The future of the second category is a glorious one. They meditate, serve, and sacrifice for the good of all humanity. These beings unfold and develop like lotus flowers, and they become more group conscious and inclusive until they eventually fuse with the group consciousness of humanity and the Hierarchy. They become bridges between humanity and the Higher Worlds, transmitting light, love, and energy to humanity.

Among them are those who will graduate from this planetary school and enter the School of Wisdom, becoming vanguards for future humanity.

The future of the third category is a dark one. Some will enter into the spheres of incessant suffering and pain. Others will be born with defective brains and bodies. Others will be forced to endure very painful experiences on Earth and in the Subtle Worlds. Their evolution will stop for a long time.

If a few seeds of goodness are found in these beings, they will find themselves in those places and environments where they will experience intense pain, suffering, restrictions, limitations, and pressures so that the seeds of goodness in them multiply and spring forth.

A few of them may lose their Guardian Angels; some of them may even lose their human souls and merge into the elements of chaos.

The greatest transgression a person can commit is to slander any Teaching which embodies all those principles and truths which are given from the Higher Worlds.

The Teaching is the Law—the *Dharma*. It embodies the living fire given to humanity for regeneration and transformation. Every act which distorts the Teaching and causes harm to the Teacher is an unforgivable slander against the Source of Light.

Christ once said, ". . .but whosoever speaks against the Holy Spirit shall not be forgiven, neither in this world nor in the world to come."[1] The Holy Spirit is the Source of the pure Teaching, the Source of Light given to humanity for regeneration and transformation.

The Teaching is the Ageless Wisdom given throughout the ages by this Source through Great Ones in different words and experiences and according to the level of those to whom it is given. Those who are touched by this spark of light will see the pure Teaching passing like a beam of light through all wisdoms and religions given to humanity. It is this beam of light that must be discovered. It is found only through tolerance, inclusiveness, love, compassion, and through a life lived for the good of all.

---

1. Matthew 12:32

Chapter Seventeen

Gratitude To Teachers

The world must be grateful for all those leaders, teachers, and gurus who have tried and are trying to keep the flame of Spirit burning. It is possible that as humans they demonstrated certain weaknesses, or perhaps they were carried away by their dreams. In certain circumstances they may have tolerated the failure of principles in themselves or in their followers. But because of their experiences, failures, and successes, they were trained to take more responsibility in the future and the Torch was carried on.

In some cases those who initially entered the path of service with self-interest became the most sacrificial persons who eventually devoted their entire life to raising the spirituality of others and to meeting the mental, emotional, and physical needs of others.

It is very easy to criticize a Carrier of the Torch, but one must also know that such Carriers often bring the most precious gifts of life. Those who criticize and look down on modern spiritual teachers, workers, and leaders—emphasizing that real Teachers existed only in antiquity and that They were the only dependable ones—have not yet read history with any real understanding. There was not a single spiritual Teacher in the past who was not attacked by his contemporaries. Even Pythagoras, Socrates, and Jesus Appolonious, with all Their purity, were not able to escape from the hands of murderers.[1]

There are people who still criticize our spiritual Teachers and condemn Them by using their own personal measures as reference. Certain philosophers and preachers look down on and insult every effort that contemporary Teachers are making to carry the Torch of Vision forward, little realizing that without such efforts, our world would sink into darkness.

Real philosophers do not condemn any religion or any church but patiently wait for the results and notice how—through all religious, metaphysical, or New Age activities—people are nourished, how their aspirations are kept alive, and how the Torch of Vision is kept burning. It is not a noble act for a church to attack another church, for a group to attack another group, for a leader to attack another leader, or for a teacher to attack another teacher.

The greatest servers are those who are more inclusive, more sacrificial, more loving, and more understanding. But how can this "more" be achieved unless one starts with "less" and slowly learns his lessons, sees the Path and the Purpose more clearly, and eventually turns into a leader to trust?

We must remember that not even a man of trust can protect himself from attacks, slander, or even from treason. We have seen many thieves in positions of authority judging those who have merely taken things to meet their needs without hurting others. We have seen many official criminals condemning those who accidentally fall into crime. I once read that a leader who had murdered thousands became a judge—and in

---

1. For further information about Jesus and Appolonius please refer to *Christ, the Avatar of Sacrificial Love* by Torkom Saraydarian (Agoura, CA: Aquarian Educational Group, 1974), pp.74-82.

turn also murdered those who wanted to expose his crimes.

Condemnation is a sign that something is rotten in the heart of the one who condemns. We must express gratitude to all those who create group visions and bring us the great ideas of the Teaching. Gratitude must also be extended to those who distribute, share, and plant these treasures and visions in different places through their speech, tireless labor, writings, songs, music, art, and so on—whether present or past. Seeing the personal weaknesses of such laborers must not prevent us from being grateful to them for the work they have accomplished.

There is another danger on the Path. People, after reading a few books and associating themselves with a teacher, slowly develop some kind of sickness which can be called "Everyone is Stupid Except Me." When a person contracts such a disease, he begins to

1. Develop ego, vanity, and separativeness.

2. Criticize.

3. Create disturbances through his thoughts in the group to which he belongs.

4. Isolate himself and sometimes resign from his membership or position just to give the impression that he is "somebody."

5. Plunge into the form of life he used to live before he entered the Path. Such people fall into previous vices deeper than before. My father used to say, "A star falls deeper into the mud if it is thrown down from a higher altitude."

If a person contracts this sickness, he must sincerely study himself in the light of the following seven standards: Beauty, Goodness, Righteousness, Joy, Freedom, sacrificial service, and striving. If he comes to his senses and realizes how he neglected to see the value of others, and if he starts feeling humble, then there is hope that he can once more try to fit into a group of people who are really trying to overcome their limitations and hindrances and stand in a purer light.

Those who catch the sickness described above show signs of the sickness long before the sickness really gets them. Once my Teacher and I were sitting on a high cliff watching the valley below. Suddenly, my Teacher pointed to six people sitting in a meadow and said, "It will be interesting to watch them." "What are they doing?" I asked. "Watch," he said, "they are drinking." He was very curious and looked pleased, as if he had discovered something new.

Ten minutes later one of them got up and started walking away, and after going about half a mile he fell down—on his face. The others did not care about him. A short time later, a few of them began to try to walk, faltering and trying to hold their equilibrium. They too fell down.

One of them walked toward us. But before he reached the cliff, he fell down. "Did you see what happened?" my Teacher said. "In sitting on this cliff we could see how it started, how it continued, and how it ended. And we can now imagine what consequences their actions may bring to them." Then standing up, in sadness and in preparation to continue our journey, he said, "One part of us must always be on the cliff in order to see what the monkey personality is doing below. Let us go."

Before people fall on their faces, they show the symptoms of their sicknesses in their conversations, interests, inclinations, expressions, behavior, looks, manner of walking, and smiles. Sometimes it is so pitiful and painful to see that they are going to fall and not have the ability to help them realize it.

One of the ways to defeat yourself and fall into the pit of vanity is to exaggerate your honesty and beauty and strongly condemn the faults of others. This is a very dangerous game. On one hand you build a "good" image of yourself in your consciousness; on the other hand you plant into that image the ugly image of the person you are condemning. The "good" image becomes nourishment for the "bad" image in your consciousness, and you will gradually become the image that you condemn.

Those people who succumb to artificial change in their life, feeling that they are now the saved or chosen ones, begin a practice which is typical to such people. They continually keep themselves busy condemning others and finding fault. By observing the lives of such people, you will see how they eventually inject the faults that they condemn into their own lives and slowly degenerate under a blanket of holiness, which does not last long.

Those who achieve greater heights become extremely careful not to find fault with others or point fingers at them. Rather, they keep themselves busy in joyous labor—seeing the seeds of beauty in others and cultivating those seeds with all their love and labor. It is through such an attitude that the faults of others are

not given the power to contaminate the laborers' consciousness.

People's measures are equal to their freedom. The
freer a person is, the more inclusive are his measures,
and he has a consciousness that is sensitive to the
essential beauty in every man.

Compassion in practical life generates an urge to
eliminate the suffering, pain, and problems of other
people, to provide them with principles, laws, and rules
which bring them health, happiness, prosperity,
creativity, and achievement.

Pity is nothing but feeling sorry for those who suffer.
Feeling sorry does not help people. But compassion is
an active labor to remove causes of suffering and help
people keep from re-creating the causes which bring
them pain and suffering.

It is very interesting to note that when we are
engaged in slander and malice, or even in treason, we
pretend to be very different from what we are, as if we
were dressing ourselves up to play a role in a drama.
This is very true in life because our real essence cannot
engage itself in something ugly unless it changes the
image, making it something else to justify those actions.

Some people use alcohol or narcotics before committing a crime so that they can be someone else,
something other than what they are. The "something
elseness" gives them an excuse to do what they want to
do. If this is understood, it will be easy to stop oneself
from committing a crime before it is too late.

The main thing to do when you find yourself under
such temptation is to try to realize what you are in
reality and try to see what acting you want to do. Such

a simple observation will warn you not to identify with the action and fall into your own trap.

In everything we regret, we see this pattern of becoming something other than what we are.

Chapter Eighteen

The Teacher

Those who teach the Ageless Wisdom try by all possible means to make their students grow and evolve to such a degree that the students take their education and field of service into their own hands.

Every Teacher plans to make his students self-propelled. He wants his students to find the source of energy within themselves and, through self-initiated efforts, increasingly reach higher states of consciousness and serve in greater fields of service.

Initially the instructions are systematized along definite lines, but when the students advance, the Teacher gradually leaves them free to take their spiritual education into their own hands.

There is a tendency in students of the Wisdom to hang upon their Teachers and on a group to secure organized sets of study. They think they need formal, well organized sets of the Teaching to help them to advance and grow.

There is nothing wrong in such an attitude at the beginning of the Path. However, such an attitude must not prevent them from exercising self-exertion and striving.

At intervals the students must be left alone, as if no one were interested in them. If they have the urge to discipleship, they will make every kind of effort to plan procedures for themselves and follow them in detail.

Self-made efforts are sometimes better than the encouragements given by others.

When the students advance enough, the Teacher must not present any study course; he must even stay cool when a student tries to force his desire to lean on the Teacher.

Many students are inflamed by outer influences or by self-interest. The Teacher must look for the true urge for striving and tactfully create certain obstacles to the flow of the students' desire for study in order to increase the current of their desire and to stabilize it.

Sometimes it is even necessary to neglect or ignore any kind of application for study from a student in order to find out how sincere he is and how strong is his urge to learn and to be. Welcoming anyone who knocks at your door leads you to failure.

Sometimes you will be able to say to your student:

"I am busy for a while; come later."

"Go and study with others."

"Why do you want to study with me?"

"I want to see you in two years."

It is important also to cause difficulties during the period of a student's studies.

Do not create close ties with your students. That will be a great mistake. Do not run after them; let them come to you and force you with their solemnity and sincerity to help them on their path.

Some teachers are excited when anyone comes to them and says, "I am ready. I want to learn. I want to cultivate my own potentials. I want to know the Teaching."

An experienced Teacher sees how such a person is unfit for the Teaching and can even be a danger in the field of the Teaching.

The reason for this is that the applicant spoke only about his self-interest. He wanted to learn, he wanted to know, but he did not say for what reason.

The goal of the Teaching is not to fill your mind with information, knowledge, or data, but the goal of the Teaching is to make you a self-sacrificial servant of humanity.

If your main reason to learn is to feel great and to use the Teaching for your own advantage, it is better for you if you wait until your ego and vanity are dissipated.

Every Teacher must be careful of those who use the Teaching for their own self-interest because the traitors of the Teaching come out of the ranks of such people.

"Why do you want to be in the Teaching?"

"I want to be smart and learn to see things as they are."

"I want to be healthy, happy, and prosperous."

"I want to be able to influence people."

All these words can be the words of a dark serpent. The Teaching starts for a person from the moment his heart bleeds for the pains and sufferings of people, and he feels the urge in his spirit to sacrifice himself for humanity.

It is true that meditation develops the mind. It is true that meditation makes you have control upon your emotions. It is true that meditation produces a healthier body.

Meditation also makes you sensitive, able, courageous, daring. But all these gifts or qualities can be used for your own separative and selfish interests. Meditation is useless except when it is inspired by sacrificial service.

A Teacher must be careful not to give wisdom to those who may use it to create barriers, cleavages, antagonism, hatred, competition among people, or to manipulate people for their own advantage.

Once my Teacher, while refusing to admit a person into the monastery, said, "If you stay out of the Teaching it will be better for you because in your case the Teaching will nourish the beasts that are within you."

For my Teacher fear, anger, hatred, jealousy, revenge, slander, malice, and treason were beasts, and he had pretty good eyes to see them in a human being and, surprisingly for me, he had the wisdom to make people see the beasts within themselves.

Another time he said, "Look at that man. He is nourishing his beasts as a pig nourishes its babies."

It is so interesting to see how we nourish our beasts—and enjoy doing it—until our beasts destroy us under their hooves.

It is interesting also how some people nourish those who nourish their beasts.

Those who approach the Teaching can have all kinds of vices, but still they can enter into the Temple if they have compassion in their hearts and the urge to sacrifice their life for the upliftment of humanity.

These two lights will never let them be devoured by their own beasts, but these two lights will give them power to surmount all weaknesses and obstacles and become worthy participants of the Teaching.

We must always keep in our minds that the purpose of the Teaching is to awaken the Divinity sleeping within us.

The purpose of the Teaching is not only to awaken the sleeping Divinity within us, but also to give us all the needed wisdom to actualize it through every moment of our life.

The purpose of the Teaching is to make people live as radiant sons of God on Earth.

Teaching From Seven Levels

A person talks on the level where his consciousness is focused. When a Great One talks, He talks on seven levels. In contrast, a person focused on one level talks only one-level talk, which means that what he says is understood as it is given, although a multi-dimensional person is able to see many dimensions in that talk if they exist. And, when a multi-dimensional man talks, the talk has multi-dimensions, which means you can translate his talk on as many levels as you are conscious on.

For example, when a seven level man speaks about food, he means seven kinds of food which you eat physically, emotionally, mentally, and so on to nourish your bodies.

To feed the mental stomach, for instance, means to give knowledge. The spiritual stomach eats foods called wisdom, freedom, joy, bliss, and so on. Your inspiration, knowledge, and wisdom are as much food as the bread you give to others.

When a seven dimensional or multi-dimensional talk is given, but you hear it from the interest of your one dimensional being, you do not understand exactly what the speaker was saying to you. You understand it only on the level where you are. And, if you try to emphasize only what you heard and say that that is what he meant, you destroy the entire idea the person was trying to impart.

If a seven dimensional man and a one dimensional man talk on the same subject, even using the same words, you will understand what they say on your level. If your level is multi-dimensional you will not like what the one dimensional speaker said because he will not nourish your other levels.

The first man will expand your consciousness. The second one, though speaking the same language, will dull it. It is not the words that convey your dimensions and multi-dimensional meanings, but it is your voice, the electricity and meaning transferred through your voice.

One person talks to all your seven "ears." The other talks only to your physical ear. When you hear even on one dimension a talk given in seven dimensions, your spirit feels content, satisfied, and happy, and you feel that there is a deeper message than what appears on the surface.

If a Teacher has three, four, or five levels, you feel them and you feel satisfied. But if you have one level and no sensitivity, you remain unconvinced and dissatisfied because your other levels do not get any nourishment. Thus your conviction depends on how many levels you have.

Our voice reflects our state of consciousness. The voice of the Teacher reflects his levels or the planes on which his consciousness or awareness is active. It is mostly through the voice of the Teacher that we understand the deeper meanings of his words.

Chapter Nineteen

The Voice

Our voice reflects our state of consciousness. Our voice also reflects the condition of our body. This is not a reference to breath. Breath, of course, contains many signs of diseases or health. But the voice is an extremely important factor by which to recognize the total condition of the body.

In the future many devices will be found to analyze the human voice and find out the real condition in which the body exists. It will be possible to find the location of any trouble in the body, diagnose it, and even learn the needed remedy through listening to the voice!

Through analysis of the voice, it will also be possible to discover the emotional conditions of man. Every emotion changes the voice. A happy voice is different from a sad voice. Fear has a different voice than hope. Anger has a different voice than love.

If people pay attention to the voices of people, they can learn great secrets about them.

It is also possible to discover the mental condition of a person by listening carefully to his voice. Lying has a different voice than the voice that speaks the truth. Confidence has a different voice than doubt.

If one knows the object about which he is talking, his voice is different from a person's voice who is imitating or showing off or repeating about a subject that he has no mastery of.

The voice reveals if one has vision, enthusiasm, insight, or foresight.

You can also hear the difference in the voices of those who believe in the things they say and those who say things they do not believe.

There are also differences between the voices that are physical, emotional, and mental in nature.

In addition, there is the voice of an integrated personality and a voice that comes from the heart. There is the voice of the human soul and the voice of the Solar Angel.

If you learn how to listen to the voices, you will hear sometimes the voice of the person mixed with the voice of a possessing entity. You may also hear only the voice of an entity who completely possesses the person. In such cases, though they may say the same words, their voices have a different pitch.

One may learn the science of voice by

- keenly listening to the voices of people

- keenly observing his own voice

on different occasions, under various conditions and moods, and thus gain first-hand experience.

Every voice has its key color and also modifications of other colors. If one has higher clairvoyance, it is possible to see the differences in color. An artistic clairvoyant easily sees the patterns in a voice and is able to diagnose the condition immediately.

Not only must we learn the condition of a person through his voice, but also we must try to see the effect of the voice of others upon our own health, emotions, thinking, and creativity or inertia.

There are voices that carry destruction through their currents, no matter what kinds of words they use. There are voices that disturb your mind, burn out your enthusiasm, dry up your creative spirit, and reverse your positive emotions.

Some voices bring healing and happiness to you; others bring misfortune. Some voices attract Angels; others, evil spirits.

Sometimes, after a stranger or a friend leaves your home, destruction, fights, misunderstanding, and confusion set in. Sometimes the opposite happens. You can decide what to do with those who visit your home after considering the results of their visit.

From this you can see the importance of secrecy in certain circumstances. For example, when you speak your secret to others, they can destroy the formation of the project before it starts to materialize itself by verbalizing it through their voice. They may destroy the project in such a way that it dissolves. It is not their words that do this but their voice.

A man spent twenty thousand dollars and created the blueprint of a machine. He kept it a secret until the last day when he was going to take it to a factory to build it. A half an hour before leaving, a friend visited him. After ten minutes of conversation the friend left. When the friend left, the man destroyed the blueprint and his future was lost.

You may have wonderful friends, but suddenly they will change. If you can find with whom they were conversing, you will find the reason for their change.

I noticed that a few times my Father would hang up the telephone on a caller, and my Mother would suggest to him that it was not a very nice thing to do. Eventually, my Father explained, "The person's voice gave me a headache, sometimes turned me negative, sometimes even made me feel nauseated."

One day the man about whom my Father was talking was found guilty of killing old people and robbing them of their belongings. When Mother gave this news about the man, Father said, "That is the same man whose voice irritated me."

Listen to those who slander and who lie. Listen to those who commit treason. Listen to the voices of those who gossip or tell ugly stories about others. You will find them very interesting and in the meantime very disturbing.

A slanderer can change the whole course of your life—not through his stories but through his voice. Even if you do not believe what he says, his voice hits you like lightning and pours poison into you from which only courageous ones can escape.

Changing your voice artificially or by exercises does little to change you or to impress others.

In order to change your voice and make it a source of health, happiness, prosperity, and enlightenment, you must change your consciousness and fill your heart with compassion and beauty.

In order to change your voice you need to have lofty visions, harmlessness, and a spirit of cooperation.

In order to change your voice, daily you must try to improve your relationships with people.

In order to change your voice you must learn to forgive others and yourself, you must serve those whom you hurt, and you must "resurrect" those whom you "killed." When hatred and malice are in your heart, never expect to change your voice.

The Voice of God created the universe. Your voice creates your future. Let your voice flow like the streams of water from high mountains and bring life, happiness, joy, and enthusiasm to all that it touches.

You may ask, "What about if people speak to relate their plans, emotions, and thoughts? How can one find the reality behind their words?"

The secret of the voice is in the existence or absence of psychic energy.[1] The less psychic energy is found in the voice, the more dangerous is that voice. Remember that the voice creates and also destroys.

Similarly our writings are charged with psychic energy or with the crystals of poison. If a person is highly clairvoyant, he can see the color of psychic energy in the sentences and on the pages. Also, he can see the fading of psychic energy or the scattered crystals of poison on the pages.

These can be detected on handwritten manuscripts better than on typewritten or printed letters or writings, though these latter also carry the psychic energy or poison to a certain degree. Our signatures carry very definite signs of psychic energy or poison.

Those who read handwritten letters and try to determine the characters of people are forerunners of those who, in the future, scientifically will prove the relationship of script with psychic energy or poison.

Some sensitives feel the contents of a letter before they open it. This means, then, that the whole man is visible if people only have eyes to see.

A girl once worked in an office with five other girls. She was educated and had graduated from college, but the other girls always felt irritated during her conversations.

---

1. For further information regarding psychic energy, please refer to *A Commentary on Psychic Energy* (West Hills, CA: T.S.G. Enterprises, 1989), and *The Psyche and Psychism*, Chapter 25, both by Torkom Saraydarian.

The business of the office slowly decreased, and the boss was forced to dismiss this girl since she was drawing a big salary and he could no longer afford to keep her.

Two weeks later, everything in the office began to change and the business improved to such a degree that the boss needed to hire two other employees.

One day a friend of the boss asked why he did not re-hire the former employee. He answered, "She was a disturbing factor in the office, and now she is slandering all her former friends and me. I do not want to ruin my business."

One voice in a multitude can bring disaster if the chance is given to it. But the interesting thing is that those whose voices carry poison, disturbances, irritation, and mistrust gradually destroy their own psychic energy and demonstrate

- stupidity
- insanity
- nervousness
- seriously damaged health

In the future, doctors will diagnose illnesses using the voice of a patient and, before it is too late, will be able to take preventative steps to change the patient's consciousness and attitudes toward life.

A poem about the voice says the following:

His voice was like the elixir of life.
His voice was like
colors of wonderful
and fragrant flowers.
                    His voice was the
                    healing breeze
                    of my heart.
Through His voice
I saw my God.
Through His voice
I saw my future.
Through His voice
I felt wholesome.
Through His voice
I reached to the stars.
                    It was a human voice,
                    so clear, so sincere,
                    so harmonious that
                    even when he scolded me,
                    I felt the cracking
                    of the walls
                    of my prisons.
His voice brought to me
light,
wisdom,
beauty.
                    His voice tuned up
                    my harp,
                    and brought me
                    the chalice of joy.

It is possible to observe one's own voice in various circumstances and conversations and find out the source of the voice.

- Is it the body?

- Is it the emotions?

- Is it the mind?

- Is it the voice of the personality?

- Is it the voice of the human soul?

One of the goals of the human being is to converse as a soul.

Sometimes people can stay for one moment in the soul, then slide down to their stomach or sex centers, or fall into the caves of hatred, malice, and self-deception.

But some people stay a long time on the summit of their soul. And a few people never come down from that summit. Their voice—either speaking, singing, or warning people—brings the refreshing vitality of the mountains.

In the voice of the Teachers of the Ageless Wisdom, you feel not only the melodies coming from a certain level where their consciousness is found at that particular moment, but also you often feel the symphony of their voice which is multi-dimensional, bringing light and beauty from the depth of their Divinity.

It is such voices that not only heal human hearts and enlighten human minds but also bring peace, balance, and equilibrium to the world.

Chapter Twenty

How The Teaching Affects Life

A Great Teacher says that the Teaching must be practical. Because of its practicality, the Teaching is accepted. If it is not practical, the Teaching is not accepted in our life. It must be practical so that we can use it everyday to make ourselves healthy, happy, prosperous, and creative. These four things are important for our life, and we can be successful if the Teaching given to us is practiced.

If, for example, a teaching is given to us that we cannot use in our daily life, what is the use of it? It creates imbalance in our system and makes life very difficult. So, the first thing that we are going to do is watch if the teaching that is given to us is practical; and, if we use that practical teaching, is it helping our health, happiness, success, prosperity, and creativity?

The Teaching is not psychology, philosophy, nor religion. The Teaching is a body of practical rules that is derived from the Laws of Nature. If you follow the Laws of Nature, you become successful. So the Teaching is nothing else but the Laws of Nature, and the Laws of Nature are explained in our consciousness by our common sense. This means we can say that the Teaching is nothing else but common sense.

What is common sense? Common sense is the application of the Laws of Nature to make yourself happy, healthy, prosperous, and creative. So if you hear anyone speak about the Teaching, the first question will be: "Can this teaching change my life and improve it?" If the teaching cannot improve your life and make you a more efficient person, that teaching is the wrong one. It is not the Teaching.

Here we have twelve practical rules, and if you carefully follow them you will see that they are very useful in your life. They will change your life in your office, in your home, in your society.

1. Try to do all that you are doing as perfectly as possible. This rule is really the foundation of success, the foundation of prosperity, the foundation of right human relationships and creativity. Everything that you do in your life, try to do perfectly, as perfectly as you can. Then, whenever it is perfect, a little later say, "I can do better than this!" because perfection is progressive.

For example, you are writing a letter. Write the letter as perfectly as you can. When you are shining your shoes, make them really beautiful! If you are cleaning your bathroom or dressing your child or teaching something, make your action really perfect, as far as you can. And always, after you do something, be unsatisfied. Satisfaction is the grave of the soul. Never get satisfied! Say, "I can do better!" If you are making a dress for yourself, make it really perfect! Make it so good that you like it. After you like it, raise your consciousness and say, "I could do it better!" This is the Law of Progress.

You get fired from your office, from your job, because you do not do things perfectly. Life is like a big factory in which we are employees. If life sees that you are not doing well in your job, it kicks you out. It is not your boss that is kicking you out; it is life that is kicking you out. Therefore, try to be in everything as perfect as you can, and then be unsatisfied, so that you improve yourself. If you follow this rule you will see a great success in your job and in your relationships.

For example, if you have a girlfriend or boyfriend, sit down and say, "Can I improve my relationship and make it as perfect as possible?"

What are you really doing? Actually, the prototypes, the perfection of everything, is within your consciousness. By improving things and making them as perfect as possible, you are bringing the perfection that is hidden within you into manifestation. You can see that the law is very simple; beneath it there is the iceberg that you cannot see!

The Teaching is the process of bringing out into your life the perfection that is like a seed sitting within your own consciousness. For example, let us say that there is a seed of a great flower in your consciousness. The Teaching tries to bring that seed into bloom in your life. If this is not happening, then everything that is told to you or you are reading is nonsense from beginning to end.

2. Do not hang on others, but provide for your own needs through your own labor. People hang on others. People expect things from others. People hope that someone will help them. Don't! Depend on yourself. See your needs and try to provide for them instead of hanging on others. This is so important! Hanging on others creates real tension in any sort of relationship, including friendships and families. For example, the husband comes and says, "Rub my feet." One day, two days, three days, four days, five days; one hour, two hours, three hours, four hours. . . . The woman becomes sick of it! We demand these kinds of things.

"Make a cup of tea for me!" Well, you make it. Stop hanging on others. You can find maybe five thousand examples in your life of how you are hanging on others without knowing it. From now on, you are going to be so alert to catch yourself the moment you are hanging on others.

What does hanging on others do? First of all, it weakens you. It makes you a dependent human being, and when you depend on others you do not grow. Every seed must grow by itself—helping others to bloom, but not depending on others. If you want strength, if you want to be successful in your life, slowly try to practice this spirit of not depending on others. Do you see the beauty of depending on yourself?

What happens when you depend on yourself? You slowly, slowly dig out the potentials that were hidden within yourself and were not used. You will be surprised how you can do much better than others if you awaken the potentials that are within you. These things are not spoken of in your universities and colleges. That is why more of our youth wander in the streets, depending on something nebulous that will come into their lives and make them millionaires overnight and very happy! That is not the case.

Everything that you have, everything that you are going to have in the future; everything that you are and that you are going to be in the future is the result of your independent actions and striving. This is so simple. This is common sense! But can you *do* it? That is the deepest Teaching. Depend on yourself. Meet your needs through your own labor.

"Daddy," a seventeen year old says, "Daddy, give me thirty dollars, fifty dollars, two hundred dollars, five hundred dollars!" Well, go work. Make some money.

Stand on your own feet and feel that you are a proud woman or man, girl or boy. Hanging on others creates rejection. When asked again, again, and again, what is asked for will be rejected.

Sometimes fathers and mothers and friends try to make people hang on so that they exploit them. Think about that. You should immediately watch that when a person says, "Here is fifty dollars," or "Here is thirty dollars," he may exploit you in the future. Be careful! He could be trapping you! Do you see that? This is the Teaching of life.

3. Economize your energies. This law is for young people and old people: Those who waste their youth in excessive pleasures pass their old age in poverty and sickness. You have five thousand dollars, but you waste it, so you do not have money to live on in the future. Likewise, your energies—your body, your emotions, your mind, your brain—are your capital. If you are wasting these things, you are not going to have future capital to use when old age comes.

I remember my father once took me under a tree and said, "Never forget this. When you are young, live like an old man so that when you become an old man, you live like a young man!"

How beautiful it is when you pay attention in your youth and do not waste yourself—your money, your energy, your mind, your emotions, your spirit, your psychic energy. You are thus saving the precious energy of life to use in time of necessity. All these are energy. Saving your energy and using it creatively brings you happiness. Wasting it leads you to sickness, unhappiness, and defeat. Everyone of us knows this in our heart.

Do not misuse your energy. Save it. Economize it without being stingy. Use your reason and logic to use energy if it is necessary. This is so important.

4. The fourth law is related to the third one: **When you are young, think about your old age.** That is also important. What are you going to do in your old age? Few people think about this until they become old. Then they start thinking and panicking. Instead, start when you are young. Think: How can I make my old age really beautiful? Really healthy? Really prosperous and a blessing for others?. . . And, when you are older, think about a possible future birth.

You are leaving this planet in a mess. What if you incarnate two hundred years later and you find the planet in more of a mess?

Think about the future. How are you going to arrange your future? People seldom think about it. Now you are here. What about your next life? What are you going to do with it? That is a very important question. You think, for example, what you are going to do the next day, the next week, the next year. Why not think about your next life!

Actually, humanity should think about the next life—whether there is a next life or there is not does not matter. Even if you think there is no next life, your children are your next life. Why leave this planet in a mess, in pollution, in destruction, in radioactivity, in poison? Your children are going to inherit that world, or you yourself are going to inherit that world. The attitude of "Today let's drink and have our pleasures, and who thinks about tomorrow?" is suicide. The people who do not think about the future will not have a future.

The Teaching says, "Without thinking about the future, you cannot proceed on the path of perfection!" When you think about the future, you have a confrontation. What are you actually doing at the present? If you are doing things at the present that will create a very complicated and unhappy future for you, you can take action and prevent things that you are doing now.

If this law were explained to the children, we would have a better humanity in fifty years time. Children seldom are taught about the future. Most are taught how they can make money now and enjoy life. If it were necessary, I would not enjoy this life if in my future three lives I will enjoy myself more!

Why not be a smart businessman with your life also? If drinking this bottle of liquor will make you happy now, but for ten days you will be sick, do not drink it! If eating this food and doing these exercises will make you not drink that liquor and will give you many years of happiness, to hell with that drink! This is a businessman's approach; you can use it in dealing with your life.

5. Do not waste your money and tomorrow borrow money from others. Do not borrow from your bank or from your credit cards. Credit cards are one of the traps that is not understood yet. Using credit cards means: You depend on others and they exploit you. That is what the credit card is.

Instead, spend your money economically so that tomorrow you do not go and beg: "Give me five dollars, fifty dollars!" People sometimes do this. They see something and get excited. They want money and they spend it, but for two or three weeks they do not have money in their pockets. What does this do to them? It makes them hate their self-image. Once you start hating yourself, you are going downhill. That is the psychological side of it.

Young men, young women, must love themselves, must respect themselves. How can you respect yourself? When you are successful, happy, healthy, and prosperous, and you love your image, you respect yourself. But if you are failing, depending on others, hanging on others, you start hating yourself. When you start hating yourself, you weaken yourself because you create short-circuits. You create a conflict within yourself or a double personality.

From the beginning it is better to teach children to economize. If you have money, spend it. But, if you are smart, spend it so that in the future you are not in a position of asking money from others.

This is how you can learn the science of economy in your life. It is a science that is written about in the little booklet *The Spring of Prosperity*.[1] It is so important. Everyone must read it at least eleven times. I have read it more than eleven times. The science of economy is the science of handling your energies, your money, your positions in such a way that they increase and make you in the future a happier and more creative person.

6. Sleep early; wake early. When you are not going to sleep early, what are you doing? List them, and you will be surprised! But if you sleep, you are in the tide of the Higher Worlds. When darkness comes, the meetings are opening in the subjective planes. Do not miss them by wasting your time in watching television, seeing violence, murder, and destruction which go into your subconscious and eventually program it and

---

1. Torkom Saraydarian, *The Spring of Prosperity* (Agoura, CA: Aquarian Educational Group, 1982).

prepare you for a miserable future life. Or you may be gambling, or talking until morning without any substance. I was in a restaurant at two o'clock in the morning after an overseas trip. Two teen-agers came and sat behind me. For one hour I heard what they were saying. I could not make out a sentence! They were just yak-yaking! I tried so hard to see if it made sense. It did not make any sense for me. I thought, "Why are they wasting their energies?"

If you go to sleep early and get up early, first of all you will hear the beautiful songs of the birds. You will inhale the freshness of the air, hear the silence, even see the stars. There is a great magnetic power and energy in the early morning.

A proverb says, "All successful people awaken early." I once worked in the British Royal Air Force. My boss was supposed to begin work at 8 o'clock in the morning, but he always arrived at 6 o'clock and prepared everything for every worker there. When I arrived, everything would be ready on my table.

Imagine a boss who is coming in at 8 o'clock and wasting the time of twenty employees! Twenty hours are wasted. And you can see this in most of our official businesses. People are coming in yawning. It is 9 o'clock and they have not started yet. When you have to take care of some business in these types of offices, it is very difficult.

If you want to organize the society and your business, know that the most successful one is the one who begins the day early.

7. Never start your daily labor, or whatever you are doing, without first praying or meditating, or at least reading something very beautiful. This mobilizes your higher forces and your soul, makes you ready for the fight of the day. You must be charged every day through your prayers and meditation. When you start every day, hundreds of obstacles and waves will come on your path, but you will be able to conquer them through the energy that you drew from the Higher Realms.

Take this very seriously! Before you start out your door, you must do your meditation or prayer. If you do not know how to meditate, how to pray, read something very beautiful. Say the "Great Invocation,"[2] at least, so that you are charged. Your polarity will change. You will become more magnetic and enlightened. Then you can have a contact with Higher Worlds, higher levels of consciousnesses. You become awakened. Prayers, concentration, meditation awaken you. Most people, perhaps ninety percent, are asleep all day long.

8. Never go to sleep without self-examination or evening review.[3] Christ once said a very important thing: "Before you sleep, before sunset, clear your accounts, your problems, with others."

Before you sleep, you are going to take a "shower." Most of you take a nice shower and put perfume on to prepare yourself for something. Similarly, you are going to take a psychic, spiritual shower. This means cleansing yourself from everything that you did throughout the day. This is so important.

Sleep is like taking off on an airplane. Before you fly, you must prepare the airplane. Those who "fly" without doing self-examination get caught up in turbulence. Sometimes they fall in their sleep and

---

2. For information on how to say this, please refer to *Triangles of Fire*, 2nd rev. ed. (Sedona, AZ: Aquarian Educational Group, 1988) by Torkom Saraydarian.

3. *The Psyche and Psychism*, Chapter 80, "Evening Review."

awaken. There is a psychic law behind this. Why do you suddenly jerk and awaken? You were caught in turbulence. There was something you did not adjust: your screws here and there, your carburetor, your steering, or something. You were caught in the turbulence, and you were thrown into your bed again.

9. Watch yourself to see if you are feeding your ego and vanity, and stop it. This is not easy to do, but you must try somehow, in some degree. Unless you do it, you cannot grow! People think they grow when they read, when they listen to lectures. They do not. You will never grow by reading and listening. You grow only when you start doing. What are you going to do? If you are thinking in a way that is feeding your ego and vanity, stop it. You may be growing like an empty balloon. If you are talking in a way that is feeding your ego and vanity, stop it. If you are dressing in ways which are feeding your ego, stop it. If you are buying things that are feeding your ego and vanity, stop it.

Vanity and ego are two destructive explosions within your consciousness and life. They destroy you. Eventually they bring you to the edge of the abyss. Those who have vanity and ego are the most unsuccessful and unhappy people in life.

If you find a really successful man, a prosperous, happy, and creative man, you will find two very important things in his nature: He has the least ego and the least vanity. He knows exactly what he is, and he knows that ego does not help. The ego is a cancer in the mental plane. Vanity is a hole in your boat.

10. Try not to impose or force your opinions and desires on others. Imposition or forcing creates reactions, creates hatred toward yourself. Let people bloom. When you are forcing your opinions and desires—especially desires—you are humiliating people. You are not recognizing their Divinity. You are not giving them a chance to grow and do things better. You are imposing your desires.

Do not impose yourself, not even your ideas. One day a man came to me and I asked him, "How are you? How is everything?" "Well," he said "I am divorced." I said, "What happened?" "Well, my wife, she is a democrat, democrat, democrat, democrat, day and night democrat! I got sick of her." Do not do that! Be a little republican, also. So what! Your marriage is more important than arguments. Let him believe what he wants to believe. You believe what you want to believe.

If there is an exchange of ideas, nicely, beautifully, in noble ways express them, backing them with reason. Then, do not force agreement because it will create repulsion. You throw out things that are forced on you. Still, you try to force others!

Eventually people become zombies around you because you forced so much that you killed their individuality, their originality! Take a girl and say, "I want you to dress this way! I want you to talk this way! I want you to walk this way!" Eventually that girl becomes a mule. She does not know what to do, and she always waits for someone to tell her what to do! You "killed" her.

11. Keep your home clean. If suddenly an honorable guest goes to your house, which one of you will not be ashamed? What if he looked into your closets? Is everything nice? Are the bathrooms organized? Are the bedrooms clean? What about the kitchen? Did you wash yesterday's dishes? That is how a neat person lives. Why is that? Cleanliness means that you have a creative influence in your home. Dirtiness, uncleanliness, disorder bring very bad spirits and entities into your home. The Teaching says: "Even gather the dry leaves and burn them," because dry leaves bring unwanted entities to your vicinity.

A Teacher once wanted to go to his disciple's house. The disciple was so proud of his knowledge, but when he found his Teacher at his door, he said, "No, not today!" The Teacher replied, "Because you said 'not today,' it is the right day for me! I will see exactly what is happening at your home!" It was a mess.

12. Try to develop humility and control over your mouth. The hardest thing in the world is to learn how much to say and what to say. But people think that it is the easiest thing.

Most of your failures, complications, and hindrances are the result of not knowing what to say and how to say it. It is your mouth that controls your future, your relationships with people, your success and creativity.

These are twelve rules taken from the Teaching. Try to apply them in your life according to what and how you understand and according to your circumstances. Teach them to your children.

Chapter Twenty-One

Working On Yourself

The Ageless Wisdom cannot be understood by reading about it or listening to it only. It can be understood and assimilated only when you apply it in your life. To do this, you must find those areas in your life which need correction and cultivation. It is through your efforts that light is drawn from your Core and expressed in your thoughts, words, and actions.

The Ageless Wisdom becomes meaningful and practical for you when this inner beam of light hits your accumulated knowledge. This means that you have to watch and observe your life and see in what areas your physical, emotional, and mental bodies need correction. Maybe you need to improve the way you walk, the way you eat or speak. Maybe you must eliminate certain habits. Then you must carefully watch and observe your emotional reactions, noting how you can eliminate certain emotional reactions which cause you embarrassment, which damage your body and mind or make you appear ugly. Next, you must watch and observe your mental activities and see which ones must be cast away as elements which hinder your progress.

This is a lifetime job, but gradually you will see great improvement in your life. Perhaps you need to eliminate vanity, control your ego, and eventually dismantle it. And along with all these labors, you must also try to cultivate and increase any physical, emotional, or mental talents you may have.

Physical talents include dancing, doing things with your hands. Emotional talents are not rare; certain people are talented in bringing joy and peace to us, freeing us from our burdens. Mental talents include an ability to teach, to simplify and explain, to share your understanding in certain branches of knowledge, the arts, and so on. You may have other creative talents. All of these must be considered and steps taken to cultivate them.

As you daily try to meet certain needs in your nature which need correction and try at the same time to cultivate your talents, you will see that your light is increasing. Your Inner Core is projecting light into your efforts and labor, and you are understanding the Teachings you study from the Ageless Wisdom.

Once your light increases, you will start living a goal-fitting life, correcting all that is false within you and cultivating the seeds of your beautiful talents. This is how the Core of light within you can be put into action so that it flows into your whole system. As it flows in, it enlightens the collected knowledge stored in your mind, bringing more compassion into your emotional world and more energy and vitality into your physical body.

Unless we are able to activate the Divine Nature within us, our knowledge of the Ageless Wisdom, even our general knowledge, will not be used for constructive purposes, for the welfare of all humanity and Nature. Without the inner light, synthesis and understanding are impossible. This light is activated and brought into our lives only through the labor of correcting certain areas of our nature and cultivating our talents.

In the final analysis, we must remember that the Ageless Wisdom is light. As the light of our Core begins to radiate and we share the treasures found in that light, the light gradually becomes a communication line between us and the higher treasuries found in Cosmic Space. Great Teachers always advise us that our light must shine—through our words, actions, thoughts, and relationships. The more light we have, the more clearly we can see areas in our nature that need improvement. The more light we are, the more we strive toward perfection.

Creativity is a dance performed to the music of light. The goal of the Ageless Wisdom is to lead us toward perfection. The steps toward perfection pass through the actualization of beauty, goodness, knowledge, joy, freedom, striving, and self-sacrificial service.

The greatest characteristic of the Ageless Wisdom is that it leads us toward inclusive perfection. It teaches us that we must carry our vehicles and their expressions into perfection.

The physical body is a Temple which must be built with perfect engineering and beauty so that it better serves the needs of the Soul—who is the king.

The emotional body must become the most sensitive instrument, with senses developed to perfection as we render sacrificial service and express joy, compassion, and detachment, keeping our emotions as pure as possible.

The mental body must be cultivated to its highest under the light of the Soul. It can unfold only when the brain is not polluted with drugs, alcohol, or various kinds of poisons existing everywhere.

The mental body has two main divisions: the higher and lower minds. If the lower mind develops at the expense of the higher or abstract mind, our evolution stops—no matter how much knowledge we accumulate in our mental memory banks.

If the higher mind is developed through abstract thinking, but lacks cooperation with the lower mind, the abstract ideas and concepts cause a person to become unrealistic, suspended in the air, a visionary who has no useful purpose in life. Such an imbalance creates severe physical problems.

The lower and higher minds must be cultivated through study, meditation, purification, and creativity. Eventually the mental body must be transformed to such a degree that the light of the Inner Light will fuse with the mental body and illuminate the mind with the vision of Life's Purpose.

In this threefold development, the person must be sure that his expression through the physical, emotional, and mental bodies reaches a state of relative perfection. This means that a person must prove that he can control his body and activities, that he is able to act goal-fittingly, economically, and with poise and beauty.

His hands, his feet, his whole body must be synchronized with his will and must act according to his creative intentions. This means that his emotional body is under control and that the automatic and mechanical nature of his emotional expressions is conquered. The emotional body is now the outlet of pure and positive emotions, such as tenderness, gracefulness, sympathy, love, calmness, and balance. If the emotional body is not controlled, it wastes the energy of the entire person through its incessant actions and reactions, which are caused by the emotions present in the environment.

The mental body can be controlled by eliminating ego, vanity, and the sense of separatism. Meditation is a technique which helps us control the constant agitation of the mental body.

The Ageless Wisdom gives various Teachings which carry the threefold bodies toward a higher standard of perfection so that their actions on the physical plane manifest perfection. The whole aim of the student of the Ageless Wisdom must be: How can I make myself ready to be useful in meeting the needs of humanity in higher and higher fields of responsibility? How can I make myself ready so that when my Master needs a service from me, He can choose me as one who adequately meets the requirements of that service?

We must know that the Universal Mind works very economically and uses every kind of talent in its proper level and field. We need only make ourselves ready for higher service. When a person is ready, his job is ready instantaneously because it is readiness that creates the job. If a person is not ready and the job requires a ready person, he cannot be hired because he is unprepared.

The Ageless Wisdom urges us to be prepared in any field, on any level. According to our readiness, our positions are formed in the field of life. Jobless people are outdated people, or people who have a psychological problem which causes them to reject and contradict themselves. They will not have a job, even if a job is given to them, because they will hate whatever it is that they are doing. Any healthy minded, "ready" person will find or create a job, even if he is laid off from the factory because it goes bankrupt.

We may say that factories and corporations fail to be successful when their systems of work or the products they manufacture and sell become obsolete, outmoded, or retarded. Not only individual employees but also the administration of a factory or corporation must strive to meet the requirements of a progressing life. This means that they need to be "ready."

There are many practical methods in life to help choose employees and co-workers. I once asked my father how he hired his secretaries, the pharmacists, and other workers at the pharmacy. He answered, "I prefer people who are pretty, beautiful, handsome, neat, and healthy, those who can do the job better than others, those who are joyful, energetic, honest, who have a sense of humor, who know how to concentrate and control their tongues, who are punctual, creative, and enthusiastic toward their jobs." Throughout the years I discovered that my father's employees were like a family. They knew their jobs and always acted with a sense of responsibility.

The Ageless Wisdom teaches us to make ourselves ready for higher jobs. Of course, Great Ones choose us, if we can meet Their needs, according to our past records. Christ once said, "Those who are faithful in small things will be faithful in greater things." This means that if a person is faithful in his small duties and responsibilities, he is ready for higher jobs.

Readiness is not only an increase in knowledge. It is also trustworthiness, faithfulness, nobility, control, creativity, adaptability, and so on—and only the Boss knows whom to choose. The Ageless Wisdom tells us that we become useless on any level where our development stops. This means that a person can be a university graduate and have a high position in his field, but he becomes "dead" if he does not further increase his knowledge and wisdom and expand his field of service.

Some of the signs that a person is making a breakthrough are as follows:

1. More honesty and nobility

2. Greater enthusiasm

3. A deeper sense of synthesis

4. An inclusive outlook on life's problems

5. An ability to see larger causes behind events

6. A disgusted feeling toward past weakness

7. Resolution for new adventures in service

Every day we must leave an outdated portion of ourselves behind. If we are satisfied with all that we are, we are living in the past, and very soon we will no longer fit the demands of life.

Chapter Twenty-Two

Access To The Source

The difference between a genius and an insane person is that, though both of them have a very sensitive psychic mechanism, the insane person has no control upon the impressions that he receives and cannot correlate them and appropriate them to immediate and distant needs. The genius can. His psychic mechanism is sensitive to higher impressions and inspirations, and he can use all recordings, correlate them with his experiences, and then use them—not only in helping the immediate need of humanity but also its future visions.

People are limited in their thinking, believing that there are Ashrams from which knowledge can be received, if only a person can penetrate into Them. This is absolutely true. But there is a Cosmic Source of Wisdom from which anyone, with due preparation, can receive knowledge, inspiration, impressions, and energy.

This Source is the Indweller, the Presence of the One from Whom all things proceeded.

Having access to this Source is having access to all sources of wisdom and knowledge, but one must make himself ready to accept this knowledge and wisdom and be able to use it in life.

Nature releases its secrets to those who have ways to use them.

What will a person do if suddenly he finds a hole in the floor of the prison in which the most precious diamonds are hidden? Of course, we think that he can bribe the guards and free himself, but what if bribery leads him to death?

Thus Nature, with all its Omnipresent Treasury, is ready to give us its wisdom and knowledge if only we make ourselves free to have the opportunity to receive and use this wisdom and knowledge to meet the needs of life.

People will teach each other less and less as their sensitivity to impressions coming from the All-Self increases.

Christ said something very interesting. He said, "It is not me, but the Father is talking through me." The problem is to come consciously in contact with that Father, Who is the same in every one of us. Once we establish such a contact, we will be an endless source of light and inspiration for others.

We also must remember that not only can we hear the "voice" of the All-Mighty Presence in us and in the universe, but also we can hear the voices of our bodies, our feelings, our thoughts, our plans, our ideas, and our visions and understand their language.

The sound of sick bodies, negative emotions, ugly thoughts, and destructive germs will be chaotic, not musical or harmonious. If our bodies and their atmosphere are polluted with blind urges and drives, with glamor, hatred, jealousy, revenge, and treason, or with illusion, ego, vanity, and separativeness, we cannot hear the clear voice of the Inner Presence.

Thus there is a price to be paid and a labor to be carried on to be able to have access to the treasury in man and in the Cosmos. When your bodies are aligned, integrated, and purified, you are an extraordinary kind of music, which the Higher Entities love to hear, and They bless the source with Their light, love, and beauty.

Harmonious emotions are those which do not contain hate, anger, fear, jealousy, revenge, and treason. When these factors exist within your emotional body, you have the reaction of your Inner Core. Your Inner Core rejects them because they are not in harmony with Its essence. Such factors are built by self-interest, which is the opposite of the interest of the Core.

When your mind is undeveloped, it is always harmonious with the Core. But when it develops to a certain degree and with increased self-interest, it creates obstacles to the harmony between the mind and the Core.

The main factors in the mind creating disharmony are the ego, vanity, self-interest, doubt, greed, and separativeness.

In Eastern philosophy, mind is called "The slayer of the Real." It is not the substance of mind that is the **slayer**. It is a mal-developed mind which rejects the light coming from the Core that is the slayer of the **Real**.

It is true that a person must create harmony between his vehicles and his Core. It is also true that a group must create harmony between members and the Core on physical, emotional, and mental levels. Such an integrated and aligned group can serve as a powerful broadcasting station of Beauty, Goodness, Righteousness, Joy, and Freedom, thus bringing great changes in society.

Geniuses are those people who are so tuned in to their own constitution that they influence their environment and cause integration and alignment. Usually it is around such individuals that groups come into existence. The individual acts as a Core and attracts the members and instructs them in the service of integrating their vehicles and aligning them to the Core. The individual stands not as an "individual" but as a plan, as a vision, as a dynamic force to encourage and inspire people to go forward to create a synthesis out of their life.

Any real Core or leader does not stand as an individual but as a representation of a plan, of a vision, and of a sacrificial labor. This is why the Core does not exploit and manipulate, does not feed his own interest, because he himself is dedicated to the work to be done.

True leaders in all ages have led people to a vision. They have sacrificed themselves for the group and for the masses of people. They, just like corn seeds, died under the earth of labor and sacrifice so that they could give birth to corn carrying thousands of seeds.

Chapter Twenty-Three

Disciples And Tests

Disciples are those individuals who try to assimilate the Teaching and actualize it in their life.

Assimilation of the Teaching increases the power of disciples and enables them to occupy prominent positions in society.

Life presents many tests to them to make them realize their worth, their readiness, and their weaknesses and accordingly adjust their life for spiritual responsibilities.

People have forgotten that the Teachers of humanity supervise and guide those who enter into the sphere of Their service. Those who demonstrate selfless striving and perseverance are subjected to certain probations and tests in order to see if they are ready for promotion in the field of their special service.

These tests are very important points for the disciple because only through tests can he prove his worth to himself and to the supervising Teachers and be ready to handle greater responsibilities.

Each period of probation and testing reveals weaknesses and potentials, and the disciple and Teachers act accordingly to make the field of service more fruitful.

Sometimes these periods of probation and testing are noticed by the disciple, and sometimes he goes through them without being aware of them. If he is aware of them, he can work more consciously to fit himself to the requirements of the higher service.

M.M. says,

> *. . .Every three years We give the disciple the possibility of expressing himself in regard to a similar event. Only according to these dates may one see the fluctuation of selfhood, coopera-tion, patience and devotion.*[1]

What are some of the tests that a disciple goes through?

There are subjective and objective tests. In his objective consciousness, under the pressure of the environment, reading and aspiration, a person changes his form of relationship with people and life in general, but often for a long time he remains the same in subjective levels.

For example, he acts honestly as long as he knows that people or authorities are watching him. But he does not act so honestly when he enters into the astral plane because he feels more free.

This indicates that the Teaching is not absorbed in higher planes by the disciple, and he has not actualized the higher principles in the subjective planes.

To find out the facts and the degree of transforma-tion of the disciple, the Teachers subject him to various tests in astral and lower mental planes, and peri-odically They watch him to see how much progress he has made or how he is fluctuating between two polarities.

---

1. Agni Yoga Society, *Hierarchy*, para.74.

These tests are carried on in the astral plane through dreams, wishes, and desires to see if the disciple is honest in the same degree as he is in the physical consciousness, or is as detached as he is in the physical consciousness, or is as devoted as in the physical consciousness.

On the mental plane, his subjective thoughts toward certain events are observed in order to see what degree of refinement he has reached in his thinking. Daily, or cyclically, or periodically, he is tested to see if he has any of the following:

a. Different feelings, emotions, actions and reactions to a similar event, to a similar object, to a similar relationship, both in objective and subjective worlds.

b. A different quality of thought regarding a similar object, situation, event, both in objective and in subjective worlds.

In the beginning the disciple is not made aware of the tests in order to avoid the excitement and artificiality of reactions and responses. But, as he advances, he begins to be aware of the operation of the tests, first vaguely, then more consciously.

After many years of probation, more awareness of the tests often makes the disciple more cooperative, more alert, and more striving.

For a long time Teachers relate to their disciples at a "distance" and want to remain unnoticed so as not to overstimulate the disciple and lead him to mechanical, artificial responses. They want the disciple to grow by his inner power to sprout and conquer hindrances; They want him to develop his latent powers.

But gradually the disciple "smells" Their presence and Their observing eyes.

The tests are related to the following:

1. To the character of the disciple

2. To his self-image

3. To his moral nature

4. To his power of endurance, perseverance, and stability

5. To his skill in service

6. To his diplomacy and wisdom

7. To his creativity

8. To his sensitivity and intuition

9. To his speed and understanding

10. To his readiness of response

11. To his skill in action

12. To his control

13. To the level of his subjective contacts

14. To his subjective and objective memory

15. To his sensitivity to the impressions coming from higher sources

16. To his accuracy of recording them

17. To his purity of emotions and thought

18. To his ability to build constructive thought-forms and to operate them in them in the right time and conditions

19. To his ability to stand under the pressures of labor

20. To his ability and skill in handling attacks

21. To his harmlessness, gentleness, gracefulness, and compassion

Of course, there are finer and higher tests to which a disciple is subjected, and they come to the disciple at the proper time to make him ready for greater usefulness.

As a disciple advances, he realizes that his life as a whole is set in such a way that it is a path of tests. He can see that the people around him, his body, emotions, thoughts, events, all that compose his life are nothing else but a well organized series of tests.

The evolution, the growth, the creativity, and the usefulness of a disciple are forged by his ability to pass through these tests in honesty, nobility, fearlessness, and with faith that the Divinity in him will eventually reach the "Crown of Glory."

Christianity translated this as a state of beingness which rests in happiness, joy, and bliss. In actuality, the "Crown of Glory" is a state of beingness in which the disciple commits himself to world service. He is tested, trusted, and tempered to go into the complicated, stormy, intricate field of world service and share his achievements with all those who have made themselves ready for the Path.

The "Crown of Glory" is symbolized by the crown of thorns on the head of Christ, when the servant of darkness led Him to the cross. There He demonstrated all that He had spiritually actualized in His life.

Disciples do not run after rest, heaven, paradise. Their rest, heaven, and paradise are the fields of sacrificial service.

They have committed their life to these tasks:

- To wipe tears
- To bring joy
- To encourage
- To protect
- To lead
- To risk and sacrifice their life
- To enlighten
- To be examples
- To create
- To synthesize
- To heal

These are the sources of their joy, and each thorn of their crown is a witness to their victory over malicious attacks of the dark ones to prevent their service in the world.

For disciples, the nature of their tests changes periodically. Periodically they are subjected to so-called tests of happiness, success, victory, position, worship, and devotion to see how much they have grown to be indifferent to these traps. Some disciples pass easily through tests of a painful nature but fluctuate in tests that are of a pleasant nature.

All these tests have a common goal: to encourage the disciple to be a useful, tempered, trustworthy servant in the Divine Plan.

On this path of tests and trials, success and failure, defeat and victory, they develop the power of detachment. The more they increase in this power, the closer they come to their True Self and the greater fusion they achieve with the All-Self.

Chapter Twenty-Four

Experience

The Ageless Wisdom comes from real experience, experience that reveals the cause, meaning, and purpose of life, but people do not sit and search for the meaning of experience. For the majority of people, all sensations or recordings of the five senses are experiences. But experience is something more than registration of sensations.

Experience means to come face to face with reality on the level where you are.

Experience means to understand the course of the event and the effect of the event on you and your environment.

You have an experience if an event was able to call forth a reality from your treasury, an idea, or a buried vision.

Higher experiences are collaborations of experiences in the past and present. Higher experiences are buried experiences within us which do not have interpretations. When a new experience evokes them and translates them, they become true experiences, and thus the inner and outer experiences coincide.

Some experiences awaken a long lost memory, a memory which is a past experience, and that memory fuses with the new experience to become a source of wisdom.

Anything one wants to do can become an experience through observing all that one is doing in detail.

As long as your consciousness is clean and your observation is sharp, any action can turn into an experience.

Unconscious actions and words become a load upon your subconscious. This is why things must not be done for the sake of doing them but for the sake of learning from them—of experiencing them.

Experiences have many levels and we can give them various names to differentiate them:

1. Accidents, mechanical experiences

2. Events which are the result of our stupidity

3. Painful experiences

4. Pleasant experiences

5. Uplifting, enlightening experiences

6. Experiences of contact with reality

7. Experiences of achievement

1. In accidents we experience pain, suffering, loss, but also we experience that we were not alert or were not prepared to avoid the accident. Often we do not even think about what we learned from that experience.

An incident turns into an experience when a lesson is learned from it.

Often a potentially great event that can be an experience is not registered as such because of its sudden nature. Instantaneous death due to an accident is such an example. This cannot be an experience because a person does not have time to understand the event and see the causes and effects.

People who have a sudden death, or remain in a coma, need someone to "awaken" them and help them realize they are dead so they can proceed on their subjective journey. Some people, however, may not want to move on but want to incarnate quickly once again.

2. We experience the result of our stupidity. Then the event becomes the result of what we had planted unconsciously.

3. Painful experiences occur when we lose a great friend or a relative or when we are involved with a friend who is full of ego, vanity, and the spirit of condemnation.

Some people want to have dangerous experiences.

We would prefer experiences that are not harmful but increase the wisdom we need to help others.

We must remember that we have had experiences while we were in the lower kingdoms which are still present in our permanent atoms.

We have had experiences in the animal kingdom of devouring each other. We have had thousands of experiences in our lives of savagery: eating, butchering, murdering, burning each other. We have had experiences of dungeons, poisonings, tortures imposed upon us or imposed by us on others. We have experiences of various kinds of genocide, wars, revolutions, and many miserable experiences that still exist on the earth. As long as human beings live in self-interest, exploitation, and separateness, painful events will continue in one form or another, and we will not have real experiences.

4. Pleasant experiences occur when our needs are met, or a lost object or friend is found, or when we enjoy nature and other objects.

Any true experience is a reaffirmation of the reality of the experience by the corresponding inner reality.

You cannot say, "I had an experience of cutting my nose," but you can say, "I had an experience of finding the reason for such an event."

It is not your physical and emotional pleasures, your pain and suffering that are the experience, but it is the understanding of the causal principles or laws, the meanings and significances that make various events into experience.

People float on the surface, and every event for them is an experience—painful or pleasant.

The event becomes an experience for us only if we can see the laws and principles operating in that event itself, which then reveals a realization from within us that our understanding of the event is true.

5. An event is an unfolding, enlightening, and uplifting experience when you can assimilate the energy, light, and revelation hidden in the experience and then transform yourself.

There are objective experiences; there are subjective experiences. Subjective experiences are out-of-body experiences in which your physical five senses are suspended while their emotional and mental correspondences are in operation.

Some dreams, revelations, contacts, impressions, inspirations, or telepathy from the subjective world are examples of subjective experiences and are treasures in our life.

Experiences are also given in many forms, for example:

- experiences in color
- experiences in sound
- experiences in rhythm and motion
- experiences in fragrance
- experiences in beauty
- experiences in joy
- experiences in freedom

Similarly, one can have objective or subjective experiences in the seven fields:

- politics
- education
- philosophy and communication
- art
- science
- religion
- economy

A synthesized experience is one that can be translated through more than one of these fields.

One can also have experiences in the particular body in which the consciousness is focused. For people who are focused only on the physical plane, all their experiences are physical. For people whose consciousness is focused on physical, emotional, and mental planes, their experiences are three dimensional. Those who are focused in higher bodies have deeper and more synthesized experiences.

The higher your level is, the more inclusive your experience is. This is just like experiencing with all your seven senses.[1] A bite of an apple tastes good to the person who has the sense of taste. But if the person has four, five, six, seven senses, the apple is experienced by all seven senses—and that is a true experience, a synthesis.

6. Experiences of contact with reality are experiences related to the contacts of your Inner Core, with the Hierarchy, and with Higher Beings.

These experiences are rare, but they indicate that your consciousness operates on a higher level, using higher senses.

Such experiences expand your consciousness and load your shoulders with heavier responsibilities in the field of service.

Those who have experience in a field of true service know that there are three very dangerous entities which destroy any kind of service:

- Ego

- Vanity

- Condemnation

Ego ties a person to his lower self. Vanity ties him to things he does not have. Condemnation ties him to the trash of other people.

The ego commits every kind of crime to secure its own interest.

Vanity creates illusions and glamors in the minds of others.

---

1. The sixth sense is common sense and the seventh is Intuition.

Condemnation identifies the person with the vices and ugliness of others and makes the future personality worse than those who were condemned.

People talk and teach through the dimensions they have. As discussed earlier, a seven dimensional Teacher speaks simultaneously in seven dimensions. His words can be translated and understood in all or some of the dimensions. When he says food, for example, he refers to the nourishing elements of all bodies—such as food, love, knowledge, ideas, beauty, freedom, bliss. Such a Teacher demonstrates the results of real experience gained through conscious actions.

7. Experiences of achievement are when you realize that you are functioning on a higher plane, with a higher body; when you see that you are able to wield energy and use it for a purpose; when you have experiences of expansion of consciousness, inclusiveness, bliss, gratitude, utter humility, utter glorification.

There are experiences you can have while you try to visit the Higher Worlds, Ashrams, or render a great service in the Higher Worlds.

You can also have experiences with negative forces and currents and even entities that attack you.

When we advance spiritually, we can in some degree choose our experiences, and, as we choose, we register conscious experiences.

Discrimination between experiences makes a great difference in saving time, energy, money, or in losing such sources of future service.

One of the items to be taught in the future to children is how to choose their experiences and not be the slaves of their karma—to choose experiences that enable them to undo certain karma from their past.

An experience can be pleasant now, but in the future it can cause pain.

An experience can be painful now, but it can turn into a joy for the future.

An experience can be joyful now, and remain joyful forever. We must try to have experiences that at least bring us joy in the future, or remain joyful forever.

So, we have three factors that lead us to a real experience.

1. The ability to see the laws and principles behind and in the event.

2. Confirmation from your psyche, your soul, that what you see corresponds to an inner realization.

3. Seeing the result and confirming it as experience.

People on earth do not have **real** experiences; that is why things repeat in their life over and over again. The signs of real experience are

1. That unpleasant, harmful, limiting events never repeat themselves.

2. That pleasant, releasing, joyful, healing, expanding events rhythmically repeat in our lives.

Real experience must teach us what principles and laws to use to avoid unpleasant and limiting events and to increase the pleasant and expanding events.

A true experience is a reaffirmation of the discovered principles and laws by inner, existing principles and laws.

One does not need to cut his head to have an experience of how one feels in cutting his head.

Experience is not a collection of feelings, sensations, pain and suffering, or pleasures, but it is the realization of the laws and principles of life in general.

For example, if you touch a flame and burn your finger, you will never try to touch the flame again. But if you touch the flame a second time, you never had an experience with the flame.

People often ask how one learns without having "an experience"? The answer is that you will never learn if you do not have a true experience. You may say, "I had an experience in which I found out the cause of such an event," or "I saw the principle working behind such an occurrence or within such a condition."

An experience is direct contact between the Causes, Laws, and Principles and the corresponding laws, principles, and causes existing within you.

You can see that most people use the word "experience" in a wrong way. An experience is an extension of your inner reality and its fusion with the similar outer reality.

Reality is the cause of events and the law governing the experience of the law in the event.

You had an auto accident and you said, "It was quite a big experience." It was not. But if you say, "During the accident I had an experience of fearlessness and protection," that is an experience.

A true experience is one that teaches you a principle, a law, a fact, a weakness that you have, a virtue that you have, a revelation through which you expand your consciousness or see the true nature of certain events and their causes.

Some people think that experience and knowledge are the same thing.

In knowledge, it is your mind that contains the knowledge.

After an experience your physical and emotional bodies share the knowledge. The actualization of knowledge is a true experience.

Knowledge cannot be an experience unless it is actualized.

People have a great amount of knowledge but very little experience. When knowledge begins to be actualized and affect the physical, emotional, and mental life of the person and the environment, it turns into experience.

There are also plans which are not based on clear knowledge but are the result of our blind urges and drives, our desires, glamors, illusions, vanity, ego, and post-hypnotic suggestions. If we actualize these plans, they turn into experiences, often of a painful nature. Here reason, logic, and the process of thinking are of great help. Through these three methods it is possible to prevent these plans from actualizing.

There should be experiences we do not want to have, and we can prevent them through logic, reasoning, and thinking.

Remember that the faculties of logic, reasoning, and thinking are the result of accumulated experiences throughout many lives.

Chapter Twenty-Five

Aspiration

The Teaching lays a heavy emphasis on the subject of aspiration as one of the tools that brings transformation in the life of people.

For example, the Teaching says,

> *Aspiration toward the Higher World is the best recourse against obsession. Thinking about the Higher World is the best proven antitoxin. Exalted thoughts not only influence the nerve substance, but also purify the blood.*[1]

Aspiration is an inner thirst which urges a person to look for a cold mountain spring. Aspiration makes him move toward the future, to transcend his level and enter a new state of consciousness.

Without aspiration we cannot expand our consciousness or refine our nature. Knowledge without aspiration is used only for selfish and destructive ends.

Aspiration is expansion of the divine nature within us. It is the expansion of our true Self. It is an urge to touch beauty, to feel Infinity and synthesis. Aspiration is the path of steady mastery over our lower self and its interests.

Our body renews itself every seven years. Every seven years we feel a new urge toward the future.

---

1. Agni Yoga Society, *Aum* (New York: Agni Yoga Society, 1959), para. 306.

Every seven years the human soul aspires. That is his cry. As the human being advances, aspiration wells up every seven years and nourishes the fields with its fresh energies until the next seventh year arrives.

An average person, even one who is lost in the traps of the world, experiences aspiration every seven years, but it lasts only a few seconds, a few days, or a few months, or it is carried for only a year and then it fades away until a new shock of aspiration is given to him by his Soul.

Group life goes through a similar process. Every seven years a new inspiration and aspiration appear in the members of the group as a whole. This aspiration manifests in the form of a new dedication, enthusiasm, sacrificial service, cooperation, and creative labor. If the group is advanced, this aspiration lasts seven years and takes on an even stronger momentum in the next seven-year period. But if the group is shallow and its membership consists of earthbound people, the shock lasts only for a few hours, days, or months at best.

It is interesting to consider why people celebrate 25th, 50th, 75th, or 100th anniversaries. Perhaps it would be better to celebrate the 7th, 14th, 21st, 28th, 35th, 42nd, 49th anniversaries, and so on because at each seventh year a person or group can charge the aspiration through anniversary celebrations, enthusiasm, and remembrance.

It would be wonderful if seven-year cycles were observed and special efforts were taken to celebrate anniversaries of marriages, groups, even nations. The seed is charged every seven years, and if this charge is synchronous with conscious aspiration, miraculous changes will be observed everywhere.

Aspiration develops an orientation in the emotional nature which is called devotion and an orientation in the mental nature which is called dedication. Aspiration leads these two powers and keeps them in the right direction. It acts as the soul for these emotional and mental powers which are used in service.

Devotion is the result of the regeneration of astral atoms. Dedication is the result of the regeneration of mental atoms. When these atoms are healthy and pure, they cooperate with the aspiration of the human soul, just as healthy cells of the body are oriented toward health. Polluted atoms or cells lead the person toward unhealthy physical, moral, and ethical conditions. Devotion and dedication are signs that a person is in a regenerative state and that he is on the path of new success, prosperity, and creativity.

When devotion and dedication slow down and disappear, the downfall of the person begins. One must be extremely careful of those who suddenly drop their devotion and dedication, like a balloon that loses its air. They not only fall into the levels of slander, malice, and treason but also cause great damage to their environment, other people, and to the object of their former devotion and dedication. This usually happens when they are attacked in the astral and mental planes. Dark forces know how to change the polarization of people's astral and mental atoms the moment that aspiration is withdrawn from the people's hearts.

This is why it is important to feel aspiration continuously through meditation, reading, and having contact with those who keep the fire of aspiration burning high.

Chapter Twenty-Six

The Art Of Meditation

The Ageless Wisdom can be understood through meditation and sacrificial service.

We are told that those who attain spiritual illumination and give a practical guidance to humanity are those who know how to meditate and how to serve humanity.

Meditation is a daily labor which must be done with willingness, joy, and ease.

It is a process of unfolding your soul-flower and radiating your spiritual fragrance.

The Ageless Wisdom cannot be assimilated except through the art of meditation and contemplation.

Meditation and contemplation not only help us to assimilate the Teaching but also help us to actualize the great principles of the Ageless Wisdom.

Many centuries ago a Master of meditation gave precious instructions on the art of meditation. He was called Patanjali.

Patanjali recommended that serious meditators do their meditation through four viewpoints, thinking on the object of meditation by considering its

- form
- quality
- purpose
- cause

These four viewpoints can be used on all kinds of seed thoughts of meditation. For example, you can use them on tangible seed thoughts, on abstract seed thoughts, or even on events and conditions taken as seed thoughts.

If you are meditating on the seed thought of "an apple," you must try to think about the **form** of an apple in comparing it with the forms of many other fruits—their shape, color, and so on.

Then you meditate on the **quality** of the apple. Quality is *guna* in Sanskrit. The *gunas* are threefold. We call them the quality of inertia, the quality of motion, and the quality of rhythm.

Inertia is equal to apathy, laziness, lack of interest, sluggishness, and to a state of death, pain, and suffering.

Motion is equal to activity, excitement, unrest, stimulation, invigoration, quickening, intoxication, inflammation, rebellion, war, and so on.

Rhythm is equal to harmony, cooperation, glory, continuity, ecstasy, expansion, blissfulness, upliftment.

The quality of each seed thought can be found in considering whether it has the quality of inertia, motion, or rhythm.

For example, let us say that a world event is our seed thought. To find its quality, we think whether this event created a condition of inertia, motion, or rhythm.

In the case of an apple, we find the quality of the apple by considering if it creates inertia within our system, leads it to motion or activity, or if it gives us a feeling of ecstasy, upliftment, and leads us to have a harmonious relationship with all that exists.

Then we come to the **purpose** of our seed thought.

What is the purpose of the apple? What is the purpose of that world event? What is the purpose of such and such conditions?

The purpose of the apple, we may think, is to provide us nourishment, to give us the needed chemistry from the earth and sun, the special elements that it has. Also, we may think that the apple itself has a purpose.

The purpose of the world event is, for example, to expand people's consciousness, to put their hearts into action, or to destroy certain crystallizations.

The purpose of that economic condition may be to make people realize the Law of Economy and the danger of falling into luxury, and so on.

Then we come to the **cause** of the seed thought.

What is the cause of the formation of the apple? Here you are involving yourself with chemistry, even with astrophysics, and so on.

What is the cause of this world event? Here you are involving yourself with politics, economy, religion, philosophy.

What is the cause of this revolution? It may be the need for freedom, or ego, vanity, self-interest, economy, power, politics, or other causes.

Thus, during such a meditation you daily expand your consciousness and the pool of your information.

We must also remember that these four viewpoints apply to all kinds of seed thoughts.

Seed thoughts can be viewed as:

- seed thoughts that are tangible or objective
- seed thoughts that have a feeling nature, such as various kinds of emotions

- seed thoughts that are in the nature of thoughts, thoughtforms, information, knowledge
- seed thoughts that are in the nature of ideas, abstract concepts, transcendental visions, and so on

But all these four kinds of seed thoughts can come under our meditation through the four viewpoints.

In reality, all of these seed thoughts have form or produce form; have quality and create certain qualities; have purpose and can evoke purpose; have a cause or causes which are projected or real. This means that these four viewpoints are applicable to all kinds of seed thoughts and to all levels of mind.

There are objects such as food, flowers, trees, odors, spices, liquors, people, any concrete forms that have the quality of inertia. They make you lazy—physically, emotionally, and mentally.

There are other tangible objects that make you act; they keep making you move continuously—physically, emotionally, mentally.

There are other objects related to emotions which make you either lazy, push you into activities, or into rhythm and beauty—physically, emotionally, and mentally.

There are mental objects that have the quality of inertia, motion, or rhythm.

The same thing is true for abstract objects. They either have the quality of inertia, motion, or rhythm.

Thus one can use these four viewpoints for the whole spectrum of existence and gradually select those "objects" or forms, directions, concepts, feelings, ideas, plans, and purposes that lead his life toward rhythm.

The greatest benefit that is gained from such a meditation is that your focus of consciousness begins to travel upward on the steps of the mental levels.

The mind has seven levels. The lowest levels are called **form** levels. Here you activate and arrange these levels through thinking on **form.**

Then when you think on the **quality,** you go to a little higher level of mind which is occupied with qualitative thinking.

Then you go to the **purpose,** and by meditation on the purpose you raise the focus of your mind to still higher levels of mind.

When you meditate on the subject from the viewpoint of **cause,** you raise your focus of consciousness to the highest levels of mind which think in terms of causes.

Thus, during such a meditation, you not only discover precious information, cultivate and organize your mind, but you also raise the level of your consciousness and begin to be a **thinker.**

Real thinking, even unconsciously, always utilizes these four viewpoints and creates a balance between form levels and abstract levels.

Those who do right meditation improve their lives, recognize these results, and strive toward greater realization.

True meditation produces ecstasy, rapture of heart. It is important to have raptures of heart in which you feel free, glorious, uplifted, and expanded in consciousness, in which you feel one with beauty. But such raptures are not healthy for your mechanisms if they do not reflect into a dedicated labor to prepare others to take such moments in their life and make their life a tool of transformation for still others.

For success, extreme tension of spirit is needed, but in each action a certain reserve must be preserved. An exhausted action loses its beauty and the magnetism of conviction.[1]

It is energy that makes our words and actions impressive and magnetic. That is why a worker who touches levels of ecstasy must not exhaust the received energy through aimless or planned activities but preserve considerable amounts of energy always so that all his activities have enough energy.

Meditation is the best natural method to create tension of spirit and lead us to ecstasy of heart.

Through meditation we develop a faculty of seeing things as they are and of refusing the things that are imposed upon us.

For example, most of the time thinking is the imitation of the thoughts of other people. We curse their opinions, ideas, judgments, evaluations, criticisms, appreciations, or refusals; we use the products of others instead of cultivating our own garden and having our own products, opinions, and measures.

Meditation makes us have our own thought, our own viewpoint.

Once a friend told me that his friends are "speakers" but not "radio stations." They are used for certain ends. And the comedy is that we often say, "This is my opinion, my viewpoint," without realizing that it is just a collection of imported ideas or viewpoints.

Meditation makes you have your own thoughts and be yourself, instead of acting as a representative of others.

---

1. Agni Yoga Society, *Heart* , para. 35.

Meditation releases you from the prisons of this or that opinion, from this or that background, education, tradition, habit, and superstition; from propaganda, politics, and other impressions, and makes you see things clearly in the new light of your mind, which you discover through your meditation.

The form of meditation is like a shining star. The quality is striving. The purpose is to learn how to think and to discover your own light. The cause is the aspiration of your soul to identify with the Soul of the Universe.

How can we find the form, quality, purpose, and cause of abstract ideas, for example, "solemnity"?

FORM

Of course, solemnity—being an expression of energy and substance—has a form, but the form is not available to us yet.

So how can we see its form? We can see its form by observing its manifestations. For instance, we can observe how a man speaks, behaves, and acts in the presence of people; how he conducts his relationships, duties, and responsibilities; how his manners, actions, and plans or relationships differ from those of a person who is not solemn.

To ponder upon these questions will be the first step in trying to find the form of an abstract seed of meditation.

Any abstract subject can be brought into tangible realms by observing its manifestation or expression.

For example:

> How does a man act
>
> How does a man feel
>
> How does a man speak
>
> How does a man relate

if he is under this or that idea, influence, and so on?

Also, we must remember that there are forms on the physical, etheric, emotional, and mental planes, built by corresponding substances, if we have the ways or means to look at them or see them. Any motion on any level creates form, and any form is the result of energy and substance.

And, we must also remember that any objective form has its subjective forms on etheric, astral, and mental planes which are somewhat different from the objective form.

QUALITY

By quality we refer again to the **gunas.** There are three gunas and their various mixtures. The three gunas are *tamas, rajas,* and *sattva,* which can be translated as follows:

Tamas is inertia, apathy, slowness, coarseness, shallowness, baseness, non-activity.

Rajas is motion between pairs of opposites, excitement, agitation, violence, pushiness, confusion, indecisiveness, ugliness, contradiction, and so on.

Sattva is rhythm, harmony, being in tune with higher principles, beauty, radioactivity, balance, purity, cleanliness, decision, etc.

Every seed thought must be observed from the angle of such qualities to find the guna that best describes the object of the seed thought.

For example, if you are doing any work for someone with the intention to retard his self-growth or cause him trouble, it is *tamasic* work.

If you are doing any work with excitement or with self-interest, it is *rajasic* work.

If you are working for someone with self-sacrifice, having in mind his higher good, it is *sattvic* service.[2]

Let us say that you are meditating on food. There is *tamasic* food. There is *rajasic* food. There is *sattvic* food. The difference is that *tamasic* food creates mental, emotional, and physical inertia in you; *rajasic* food creates excitement, stimulation in your lower centers, and makes you ready to fight or work excessively; while *sattvic* food makes you clear, creative, balanced, highly sensitive, and cooperative.

All these can be understood by the exercise and discipline of meditation.

Theoretical knowledge is not experience, and without experience one cannot understand.

PURPOSE

The purpose of the abstract seed thought is again very easy to find if you ask the question—What is the abstract object intended to do?

---

2. See also *The Bhagavad Gita* by Torkom Saraydarian, trans.

Every object is created to do various things. What is this object intended to do mainly? What is it doing now? What else can it do? What is the temporary and ultimate purpose of this object, which can be anything you can imagine.

CAUSE

How did this abstract object come into being? What is its complimentary or collective cause?

For example, take an event. How did this event come into being? What was the cause of it? How many sub-causes contributed to the main cause. What level cause was it?

- natural
- human
- solar
- cosmic
- etheric
- astral
- mental
- spiritual

Was the cause human, animal, or superhuman? Was it chemical or related to forces, energies, planes?

Was it an emotion; was it a thought; was it the result of an action?

By thinking and meditating upon these four viewpoints, you develop not only a scientific, organized mind but also a mind that can bridge the Intuitional and mental planes.

Searching for the cause of national and international events develops your political understanding.

Ask, for example, why the price of gasoline fluctuates so much. When did it start, following what action, where, and by whom?

Why has terrorism spread all over the world; what is its main cause?

A man cannot see things as they are until he sees

1. their real cause

2. their real purpose

3. their real quality

4. their real form

Some people who have meditated for years have developed a better, deeper, and more accurate thinking than those who have graduated from universities or serve special interests.

Once my Grandmother was discussing a legal question with a lawyer in our family.

She said, "But don't you see, you are making up things?"

"Grandma, how do you know these things? Did you study and learn?"

"I don't need to learn to know. I know because I know how to think clearly."

Most of our opinions are based upon the opinions of other people. Our life intention is to have our own opinions. It is not necessary to oppose or contradict the opinions of other people, but our opinions must be our own, the result of our own thinking and investigation and understanding. When we progress in meditation, we build our own opinions, and a time comes when—because our consciousness begins to work on the higher mental plane—we see the real causes, purposes, qualities, and forms of the objects or subjects and have our own real and factual opinions.

Meditation releases your mind from any preconditioned ideas and opinions, prejudices, superstitions, and glamors and helps you discover your own ideas and opinions.

Meditation insulates your thinking from the influence of the thinking of others but gives power to your mind to penetrate into real causes.

We must remember that propaganda, advertisements, politics, opinions, traditions, and fanaticism control the majority of the process of our thinking. You can surpass all these obstacles by learning how to do meditation.

Scientific observation is an observation not conditioned by outer and inner disturbing influences.

Some people think they prove that they are thinking when they oppose or contradict the thoughts of other people. This is not true. Sometimes you need to think a very long time to argue with the ideas of someone, or add a few points to them, or totally assimilate them.

In real thinking one never thinks from the axis of his ego. Real thinking dissipates ego and vanity and increases the facts for the sake of the facts.

For the beginning of your research and meditation you can use a technique which is called changing your viewpoints vertically and horizontally.

Vertical viewpoints are

- form
- quality
- purpose
- cause

Horizontal viewpoints are

- individual, conditioning elements
- family
- group
- nation
- humanity
- global
- solar

The second, or horizontal, viewpoint tremendously helps you find deeper layers of your research and in the meantime eliminate any error in your conclusions.

Through meditation, your consciousness travels from one level of the mind to another level.

For example, by meditating on the form, you travel from the seventh level of the mental plane up to the fourth.

When meditating on the quality, you use the fourth level of the mental plane.

The third level is reached through the purpose.

The second and first levels, which are truly the causal levels of the mind, are reached through thinking on the cause of your seed thought.

In meditation, time is not as important as the speed. Speed is achieved on the mental plane by spiritual tension, concentration, clarity, and psychic energy.[3] One person can meditate one hour and discover things that another person can find in one minute.

The causes of events and objects are hidden from people because their consciousness is focused on the lower levels of the mind. On the higher levels of the mind—especially on the first and second levels—all that transpires on earth is echoed or reflected. Those who penetrate into such levels can see clearly the causes of events, even when fabrications are spread to cover the real motivations.

This is a very important point to consider: **The causes of events are reflected on the highest levels of our mind, whether we are conscious of them or not.**

Enlightenment, in a sense, comes to us after we begin to see causes.

No one must sit and meditate on a wholesale basis without first having command of the causal levels of his mind. It is in having such a command that he can enter into contemplation and penetrate into the clear light of Intuition.

A person can meditate on the form and stay a hundred years in the basement of the mind.

Similarly, he can meditate on the cause only and live as a hermit in the mountains.

The secret of meditating on the four viewpoints is that we integrate and bridge every level of our mind

---

3. For further information please refer to *A Commentary on Psychic Energy.*

and make it a unified field of light, so that we are able to see the abstract as concrete and the concrete as abstract. This is how a practical idealist is created.

Grounding is as important in mental work as in electrical equipment. The causal level must be grounded in the form level, the result or effect level, to make our meditation fruitful and cause illumination.

Sakyamuni Buddha was enlightened because He saw the causes of human suffering.

Without seeing the cause and relating the cause to its effect, one cannot reach enlightenment, which is the purpose of meditation.

This technique of four viewpoints is especially good to cultivate memory. As you progress through these four viewpoints, you experience not only a sharper memory, but also you remember things that you need for certain times. Even memories of childhood and wisdom gathered from past lives emerge on the surface of your mind. Through such a meditation you develop the tools which assist you to remember and sharpen your memory: association or chain reaction, reverse association, and correspondences.

Memory is like the information stored in a computer. To be able to read the material, cooperation between the computer, the keyboard, and the computer screen is needed. If there is no cooperation between them, you cannot read anything on the computer screen nor remember anything on the screen of your mind.

Memories are in the computer. All that you have experienced is in your memory, whether you can remember it or not.

Memories, then, are awakened by three tools that have something in common with the stored memory:

1. Associations or Chain Reactions

2. Reverse Associations

3. Correspondences

1. **Associations or Chain Reactions:** For example, some years ago you were with a girl and she had used a rose fragrance. Years passed and you forgot it totally. Then you went to a class and smelled a rose fragrance, and you remembered the girl.

2. **Reverse Associations:** There is a law in the mental realms which says, "Opposites draw each other to the surface." For example, if someone is very cruel to you, you remember one who was very kind to you, or when you are experiencing hot days, you remember cold days.

If you spread good will, hidden ill will comes to the surface. In life, positive principles become active when negative actions appear in their destructive forms.

3. **Correspondences:** You remember a chair because you are sitting on a rock. You remember an airplane because you see a bird. This point can be developed further on many levels.

There is still another cause of remembering or memories. Cyclically our storage of memories goes through a period of explosions. It throws things out which come to the surface of our mind, sometimes in very unexpected moments.

The causes of such cleansing processes are many:

a. Shocks caused by events

b. Increasing light in your consciousness which creates a vacuum to draw out old memories

c. The need for karmic adjustments

Every item of storage in the memory has a code number. That is its keynote or vibration. You can only remember or call a memory out of its storage by the corresponding code number, vibration, or keynote.

It is possible to prepare a scientific procedure to draw out sleeping memories lost for ages.

Man has two additional senses which may enrich his memory. Common sense is a poor word which does not do justice to the sixth sense, but common sense means here a sense that gathers all information recorded by the five sense and creates a synthesis out of them.

Intuition is the seventh sense.

Common sense is the sense that has the ability to bring together the recordings of all other senses and synthesize them in an understanding or a conclusion or a synthesis.

There is a secret in the common sense. While other senses are related to the earth memory of one life, common sense is related to the memories of subtle planes and for many lives. That is why common sense is full of wisdom, and it may be called an inherited wisdom.

Because common sense has the ability to see objective, subjective, one life, and many life impressions or memories, its conclusions are more dependable than the conclusions of any individual sense.

The sense of Intuition, in this case, helps you open your experiences as mirrors to understand things going on in the Cosmos and relate yourself to a Greater Life.

Common sense develops as a result of your continuous and regular meditation. Intuition develops as a result of contemplation and the exercise of reading symbols and understanding the deeper meanings of myths.

Meditation makes a person not only collect knowledge from various levels of the mental plane, not only bring certain needed memories to the surface, but it also builds a new physical and psychological form, cultivates higher qualities in his nature, making the person an example, a purpose for others to achieve, and finally makes him a cause for spreading the beauty that he discovers on causal levels.

Thus, by meditating on form, quality, purpose, and cause, the person himself becomes a form more refined, develops superior quality, and becomes a purpose and a cause.

This is why we say that the technique of meditation can be learned and information about the Teaching can be accumulated in one's mind, as any information about any scientific subject, but the person remains the same brutish and inconsiderate person in his life. Without transformation through these four viewpoints, the Teaching and the technique of meditation can be used as destructively as any technique given by science.

In the science of meditation our purpose is to transform our vehicles, to transform our life, and to live as a cause, not as a tool in the hands of other persons and forces.

Only those who become causes can do things, can create a new life, can open a new path, and can help people reach their spiritual destination.

The Ageless Wisdom teaches that meditation is practiced not only by advanced human beings but also by Masters, as for example by the Buddha and the Christ, even by the Planetary and Solar Logoi. They all practice meditation in different forms and intensities in order to advance on the Path of Infinity, to be creative in Their own field of service, and to expand Their communication network with all planes of life.

Thus meditation is a science, the A B C 's of which we are trying to learn in our own level of existence.

Meditation opens the doors leading to our Divine Self and to the other dimensions of life where exist great Beauty, great Power, and great Glory.[4]

---

4. For further information regarding meditation, please refer to *The Science of Meditation* (Agoura: CA, Aquarian Educational Group, 1981), and *Psyche and Psychism,* both by Torkom Saraydarian.

Chapter Twenty-Seven

The Philosophy Of Wholeness

People have investigated the holographic pattern of cells and have reached the conclusion that "each cell contains a copy of the master DNA blueprint."

This is also true in the domain of our actions, words, and thoughts. Each thought, each action, each word that we express builds up the whole that we are. If our voice or the energy pattern of our thoughts and actions are analyzed, we will find out that their patterns are like holograms, each exactly reflecting the human ego.

The human ego is not the human soul. The DNA is not the archetype of the body. The human ego is a combination of matter and spirit, tending to become a human soul.

The DNA is the "ego" of the body, or it is the reflection of the permanent atoms in physical matter. The level of matter that spirit is focused on and identified with is the ego. The ego has the characteristics of all that the human soul has, except that the ego is not pure, and most of the time it is controlled by the matter it is identified with.

Matter is the recorder of all the experiences that an entity has through many lifetimes. It is these experiences that are used by the ego to identify with matter.

The higher the identification of the spirit, the higher the experiences it has for its own use. And, during its evolution, the spirit gradually discards all those experiences which do not fit the archetypes found in its essence.

The archetype in the human soul is a model of progressive perfection. DNA is conditioned by life circumstances or chains of incarnation. The human soul is the spirit plus the collected experiences which are in harmony with the patterns of spirit. These experiences are used as tools to solve problems of life on each level where the soul is focused.

The holograms of the thoughts, words, and actions of the ego are different from the holograms of the thoughts, words, and actions of the human soul. The difference is that the holograms of egoic activities are centripetal and the holograms of the soul are centrifugal.

Also, the holograms of egoic activities are images of the patterns of the matter aspect of man, and the holograms of the soul are archetypal patterns of spirit. Thus the human being, matter and spirit combined, is the mixture of these two kinds of patterns, which agree with or conflict with each other, creating what we call the human life in all its facets, and in each facet we see the same mixture of both holograms.

Spiritual evolution is accomplished by the spirit detaching from its identification, building a focus of experience on the higher mental plane, and using it as the base from which to lift itself and penetrate into its pure beingness in the Intuitional Plane—with all its distilled experiences.

The pattern of the human soul is harmonious, and it has a pure resonance with the Cosmic Magnet—the Galactic Soul—having the visible galaxy as Its body, with invisible vehicles behind the visible galaxy.

It is this resonance that forms the communication line between the human soul and the Galactic Soul. And these two holograms reflect within each other and challenge each other to be active on both levels, in potential or active presence.

This is why in each human soul the Galactic Soul is present eventually to manifest Its complexity through the human soul, and the human soul is present in the Galactic Soul as its womb to grow into a baby Galactic Soul.

This is the pattern in which the "above and below" or the microcosm and macrocosm work.

To guide people into the awareness of this pattern, one has to explain the interrelationship of spirit and matter, and the expressions radiated out of an ego and a human soul.

The discovery of the different patterns of expressions (through words, actions, etc.) creates all those methods by which we build measures to evaluate people's lives. These measures are actually applied to discover the soul or ego pattern in human expressions. Also, these measures are used by souls and by egos.

The difference between such use is that the ego measurement is always done by the standards of the ego, but the soul measurement always considers the standards of the greater whole and, specifically, the standards of the Galactic Soul reflected in the human soul.

It is interesting to note that man—either soul or ego—exists in all his expressions as a complete whole, and it is his expressions that will be attracted to each other (being from the same source) and create his next vehicles of manifestation.

Such a manifestation can be an egoic manifestation or a soul manifestation. If it is an egoic manifestation, it means man did not become a soul yet, and his vehicles are subject to various pressures to come into harmony with the galactic pattern. But if it is a soul manifestation, the created vehicles will be in harmony with the patterns of the Galactic Soul and will assist the human soul to further expand his resonance with the deeper layers of the Galactic Soul.

This is how an Initiate or a Master, Whose vehicles are transfigured and no darkness exists in them, comes into being.

"Darkness" is a symbolic word meaning inharmonious conditions existing in and between vehicles.

How can we sense, know, and touch the holograms of our expressions, as in every expression light and darkness exist and condition our future manifestations? The first step is to follow the philosophy of wholeness.

This philosophy is created by those Beings who were Mahatmas or great and emancipated Souls. Such a philosophy is found in the *Puranas*, the *Upanishads,* the *Bhagavad Gita*, in the Teachings of Buddha and Christ, in the Teachings of H. P. Blavatsky, Alice A. Bailey, and in the Agni Yoga Teachings.

The philosophy of wholeness, which can be understood by studying the science of holography, can guide us in our thoughts, words, and actions. This philosophy can be translated as: Whatever you think, speak, and do affects the whole existence; and all that you think, speak, and do can be the echoes of all that the whole thinks, speaks, and does.

Certain expressions of a person originate from sickness, depression, or inharmonious conditions of that person's vehicles; other expressions originate from happiness, joy, and bliss. The first type of expressions creates pain, suffering, and natural disasters. The second type creates happiness, joy, bliss, harmony, and cooperation between people and people, and between nature and the Galactic Whole.

Holographic theory also explains the patterns of the weather, stability or earthquakes, storms or good weather, natural calamities, and natural conditions of the Earth.

People have difficulty in understanding that we condition the behavior of nature through our thoughts, words, and actions.

Each thought, each word, each action is done in the circle of the whole existence. The interactions are cumulative. They have their own laws, and the moment to release their force is created by the accumulations of positive or negative expressions of the human world.

To cultivate the human consciousness with the principle of wholeness is the safest way to guarantee happiness for humanity, as well as for nature and for the galaxy.

The principle of wholeness is found in each cell, atom, and the human soul, projected by the Galactic Soul. What are the components of this principle?

1. Live for the All.

2. Strive toward perfection, which means try to be a soul. A soul is pure intelligence, love-wisdom, and willpower.

3. Expand your consciousness to understand the wholeness of existence.

4. Develop your sense of responsibility.

5. Do not deprive creatures of their lives.

6. Teach with love.

7. Consider other people to be as important as yourself and live in harmlessness.

8. Think how the Galactic Soul can be realized as your soul.

The Ageless Wisdom teaches holism and wholeness. The Ageless Wisdom teaches that all creation is a unit, and every part of it reflects all other parts and the unit as a whole.

It says that we are the whole that exists.

The Ageless Wisdom urges us to actualize such a concept in our selves.

Chapter Twenty-Eight

One Humanity And The Teaching

People talk about universal brotherhood, a time in the history of the planet when every nation will co-operate and work for each other to make the world a sane place, a place where life is happy and highly progressive. This is a great dream, the actualization of which is the vision of each human being. But what are the steps of actualization of such a dream, of such a vision?

1. Universally recognize the rights of each nation. Recognize the right of existence of their culture, language, traditions, religion, arts, etc.

2. Correct all those historic mistakes that were made to destroy a nation or a group of nations through genocide, wars, revolutions, and political pressure. This means to bring the involved parties into an agreement in relation to their borders, possessions, etc.

3. Create a universal law to prevent any aggressive action by any power against any other nation.

After these three steps, there are three other steps which will create right human relations:

1. Allow freedom to travel or live anywhere in the world.

2. Give economic help to those countries which are in poverty or in dire need due to natural catastrophes.

3. Create a one world army. This army will be under the jurisdiction and command of the United Nations, which in turn will act as the world government. No nation will have its own army. The army of the United Nations will be a police force rather than a military force.

After these three steps there will be yet another major point. Books must be written by specialists about the following:

1. How to create the spirit of world citizenship.

2. How to create the same laws for every nation in the world.

3. How to create a world supreme court acting under the United Nations to execute the law in all nations through the courts and the police force.

Unless we create unity in the world, the world will destroy itself.

It must not be tolerated for any nation to create movements and negative attitudes against other nations.

Each nation will have absolute freedom to pursue its art, history, education, and religion, provided none of them contain any antagonistic, derogatory action and thinking against any other nation in the world. The most important issue at this phase of history will be spreading the philosophy of cooperation, loving understanding, and the sense of responsibility. Later, people will be taught about humanity being one family.

Such an age is not far away from us, if we take steps to create it now.

The suffering and pain of the world has taught us to end such misery and begin to develop solar, galactic, and cosmic vision; to transcend all our past achievements and modes of living which have brought us not only pain and suffering but have also threatened life on this planet.

We can now declare to the people of the world that the time has arrived to start building the one Family of the Mother Earth.

The Ageless Wisdom urges us to respect the rights of every nation, their language, their culture. This especially applies to one's own nation. The greatest sin, according to the Ageless Wisdom, is an act of treason against one's own nation. National sanctity all over the world must be recognized and respected by law.

People must understand that the effort to annihilate each other does not secure happiness, success, and victory. Nations pay heavily for their past crimes.

No one can annihilate a soul; it will always exist. By killing a person, the problem is not solved. The only way to solve problems is by using the law and education.

It is through education that people will try to solve problems in loving understanding, and the law will protect those who are under the attacks of ignoramuses.

Humanity is ripe; nations are ripe; they are all waiting for the big powers such as China, the Soviet Union, the United States, Great Britain, and a few others to cut the ribbon to the bridge that leads to the New Age of harmony and cooperation.

The United Nations is the only hope that we have on Earth. Gradually it must take its position as the only power and guide for all nations in the world. Additionally, by giving power to the United Nations, the big powers would be bringing freedom to all people everywhere.

In the future, in such an atmosphere of cooperation and harmony, religious leaders will formulate a religion that can be acceptable to all people. But even such a religion must not be forced upon anyone because the freedom of the individual will be considered the most sacred possession of men.

In the future, religion will not function under fanaticism, superstition, or blind faith, but it will be enriched by reason and logic, by intuition, and by the effect it will have upon the relationship between people and people, and between people and the Creative Source of the Universe.

Religion will be used to solve the problems of humanity and the problems of the human psyche. It will be a scientific religion. But that scientific religion will not be imposed upon anyone either; its beauty will be revealed and its power will be demonstrated in relation to the building of human happiness on this planet.

Of course in the future, new breakthroughs will be achieved and the veil between physical existence and spiritual spheres will be revealed.

All such activities will be carried out in a truly scientific spirit and not in fanaticism, blindness, nor selfish pursuits.

The law will try to eliminate all those activities in every field of human endeavor that spread fear, use fear, and make people live in fear.

Punishment eventually will be removed and replaced by education, training, discipline, which will be organized by physicians, physicists, and psychologists.

I was following the life of a few boys who were from good parents and living in a good community, helping and serving their neighbors and friends.

One day after a party they were tempted by a boy to break into a car. It seemed exciting and fun for them. A few hours later they were caught by the police and imprisoned. The court, the judgment, the negative feelings of the people affected them so much that they swore to be public enemies as soon as they were freed from prison.

Years later they became professional thieves and gangsters and used these sorts of activities to exhaust the hatred and revenge accumulated in them.

Society did not gain through such a procedure. The boys could have been counseled and given a challenge of a great vision so that they could re-orient their whole lives toward the fulfillment of that vision.

It is not the law that heals and transforms; it is education, counseling, and good examples that not only save money and cause transformation but also help people find higher directions in their lives.

The more the laws increase in number, the more it indicates the increase of corruption. The more the laws increase, the less people have a chance to transform themselves.

Of course at this stage of human life, the absence of any law will create chaos and anarchy. But our legislators have to decrease the number of laws needed to deal with its citizens and increase the number of other methods which are less costly and can more powerfully transform the lives of people.

Churches of all denominations and faiths, all over the world, are doing a marvelous job to awaken the sense of responsibility in people and create right human relations. In so doing they are protecting the world from future problems.

Of course, certain brotherhoods such as Masonry, Rosicrucians, Theosophy, and other health and light-oriented groups are also doing a great job in transforming people's lives.

There are also wonderful medical doctors, psychiatrists, psychologists, and counselors who are helping people find a better way to live.

These successes have been based upon the solid foundation of the Teaching which enlightens people in five stages.

1. There is the most glorious beauty in every human being... ready to manifest.

2. The sense of responsibility leads to peace, cooperation, and self-actualization.

3. Regular meditation and study expand our consciousness.

4. Creativity is the ability to bring into birth hidden potentials within our nature.

5. A life of sacrificial service is the greatest
reward we can have from the Most High.

The children of the world must learn that the sum-
total of all beneficent laws is found in the core of their
heart.

A whole scientific organization must be brought
into being just to create those steps and procedures
that will make the above ideas available and ready for
the generations to come.

The more this Inner Law is discovered, the less
violation of laws will occur. Eventually people will
have no laws because they will discover the essence of
Law right within their heart.

The heart center can be put in contact with the
Cosmic Magnet, which is the Law. Once this contact
is established, everyone of us will know how to live with
each other and how to relate to Nature.

It must be understood that man essentially is good,
and if he falls into a crisis, it is because he needs repairs
in some part of his nature which has been damaged for
various reasons in the past. Such an approach will have
a greater effect on human progress than punishment
and inhumane acts.

Prisons will still exist for a long time, but they will
turn into colleges, universities, and art centers to bring
out the greatness that lives in every human being.

People will not be forced to hide their opinions and
attitudes and dreams. These must be brought to light,
free of the atmosphere of threat and fear.

A person must have perfect freedom to express his
thoughts and listen to other viewpoints, without being
afraid that people will take advantage of or hurt him.

Dialogues and discussions should be organized to illuminate and help each other arrive at a higher and more inclusive conclusion that is for the good of all.

In these discussions vanity, ego, and separative interests will not be the basis of discussion nor will they be expressed. Rather, those ideals which seek the good of all will form the basis of expression.

Will such a world be conservative, or democratic, or follow any other specific kind of philosophy? Needless to say, no matter what kind of government nations will have, their main intention will be cooperation with the rest of the world for the sake of all and in the absence of fear.

It is most probable that politicians and philosophers will sit around a table and formulate a new diplomacy which will draw from all regimes the best parts that they have, which can then be used to make humanity one family.

Creating a human family does not mean the end of our search for better ways. On the contrary, after the human family comes into existence, the intellect and the power of Intuition in man will take giant steps in studying the Laws of Existence and formulating them into laws by which man will live.

The whole existence down to the minutest atoms is governed by Laws, and we see that the Laws of Nature are successful. Why not study these Laws and apply them in human life and relationships?

After the human family has actually come into existence, the human potential will build bridges between solar systems and galaxies.

We have great works to do, once our nose is lifted from the cesspool of crime, separation, and greed.

The building of the planetary family will not materialize suddenly when hindrances which people have been feeding on have been terminated, hindrances such as separatism, materialism, totalitarianism, greed, ego, and vanity. All these will continue to exist for a while longer and create localized problems, but eventually, under the pressure of world opinion, they will slowly melt away.

To heal the human race is to establish right human relations, integrity, harmony, and cooperation. When the spirit of unity is cultivated and the principle of "I am a cell in the whole body" penetrates into our minds, it will be unnecessary to exercise vanity, ego, greed, and separatism.

By eliminating these factors, people will eliminate the major sources of pain, suffering, want, disease, war, and hatred.

Such a spirit of global harmony and unity already is dawning in the hearts of all creative, loving, and sacrificing people. The actualization of such a vision is only a matter of time.

The United Nations has collected precious experience in all these years of its existence. All governments must have the foresight to increase the power of the United Nations and eventually give all the power of the world governments into its hands. This is how we can save the world.

Observation, thinking, and meditation will be the major methods by which the youth will be trained. Through these practices, the youth will recognize the necessity of cooperation and harmony.

Right human relationships, harmony, and cooperation for the world start within our mind. The more we cultivate our minds with the vision to serve humanity, the more we will eliminate those factors that have delayed the dawning of the Golden Age upon us.

Through meditation people learn to analyze, relate, and synthesize and to build a network of light to spread the knowledge discovered through meditation.

One first chooses seed thoughts and works on them, training his mental powers to

— analyze

— relate

— synthesize

When the powers of the mind are sufficiently trained, the person uses his mind as a tool of creativity. Meditation thus helps a person to

— receive

— develop

— cultivate

— and express

his ideas.

When this training is continued for a long time, the Inner Guide begins to direct the thinking process by dropping into the mind of the person those seed ideas which will prepare the person to raise his focus of consciousness toward the higher planes of the mind. The activity of the mind assumes a new form on these planes.

The Teachers see the light shining in man and plan to train the person in a similar way as the Inner Guide did, dropping seed ideas related to humanity, the planet, the solar system, and beyond.

These seed ideas are dropped at unusual times, and the disciple must be ready to welcome them and begin to observe, analyze, relate, synthesize, and create.

With this method the Teacher uses a ready device—the person—to reach humanity and spread those lines of thought which will lead humanity into health, happiness, prosperity, and enlightenment and enable it to reach out from the planetary limits to the solar system.

A disciple's meditation becomes a way of service to the Teachers, to the One Self, and to the Soul of humanity.

Through meditation an individual will eventually reach illumination in which he will see his position as a cell in the body of humanity. This is the moment that vices related to his ego and vanity and greed will evaporate.

The highest honor of a person, the highest glory of a person, is the moment when he decides to promote the vision of one humanity, living together with others' individual beauty, and offering his own special characteristics to compose the Universal Symphony.

On the path to one humanity the greatest device is the use of freedom. True democracy provides such a device while, on the other hand, totalitarianism paralyzes all possible endeavors to freedom.

Totalitarianism imposes duties on people, makes them the slaves of labor, and tries to keep them on the same level of consciousness.

Democracy, if it is real, develops not only a sense of duty but also the sense of responsibility. The sense of responsibility unfolds the consciousness of people and enables the focus of their consciousness eventually to operate on a higher dimension which is more inclusive.

When totalitarianism collapses, chaos and anarchy spread everywhere, due to the lack of the sense of responsibility in people. People engage in acts of revenge as a result of the suppression of their rights in the past.

We can see very clearly today that the dictatorship of totalitarian governments is on the path of disintegration. There are various types of totalitarian governments in operation today, and Communism has become one of them. Without the development of the sense of responsibility, neither Communism nor Democracy can survive. The consciousness expands and unfolds only when people can exercise their free thinking and are able to stand for their rights.

Under truly democratic conditions, people's consciousnesses can grow because their life is not computerized and they have continuous challenges to use their sense of responsibility.

There are many historical examples of the disintegration of armies and nations as a result of the totalitarian suppression by their own governments.

Group consciousness, or the tendency to live for the interest of people and contribute to the Common Good, cannot develop under totalitarianism. This is why, when totalitarianism collapses, the people attack each other to try to regain all that they had lost while being suppressed.

The sense of responsibility begins to develop within us when we receive flashes of feelings that human beings have a common principle within them, and that

> *the sons of men are one*
> *and I am one with them.*[1]

Totalitarianism develops the germs of its own destruction.

---

1. From "Mantram of Unification." For complete prayer, see *Five Great Mantrams of the New Age*, by Torkom Saraydarian (Agoura, CA: Aquarian Educational Group, 1975).

Chapter Twenty-Nine

Three Kinds Of People

It is very important to know what we are, what other people related to us are, and what we can be. If these three things are clear in our mind, then we will have a base upon which to function. But if we do not know who, what and where we are, what other people are, with whom we are related, and what we can be, our life becomes a life of confusion and failure.

When a person does not know what he is, all his thoughts and actions have no foundation. He thinks and does things by imitating others, or he is controlled by others. This is true even in business life. If you are a carpenter, you do carpentry; if you are an electrician, you do electrical wiring; if you are a mason, you do masonry. But if you are a nobody, you try to do those things which do not require any specialization. One must know what he is and what he can do. Your "doingness" is always based upon your beingness.

We must know what we are, and then what we can and cannot do—even if we want to do it. Physical, emotional, mental, and spiritual beingness conditions what we can do on the various planes and conditions how these planes can help us do things properly on any plane.

Things are done by you or through you. Things that are done through you do not belong to you; things that are done by you have their cause in your beingness. If a person has no specialization or beingness, then other people will decide what he is to do. For example, if a person hires you for eight hours a day to do different kinds of jobs, in this situation your employer gives you a duty, a beingness, and expects you to do what he wants you to do.

Your thoughts, words, and actions must be founded on fact; this is beingness. If a person does not like the facts of his beingness, then he can change them if he works hard.

It is also important to know about the people with whom you are related. If you have a beautiful boat but do not know the condition of the ocean, you may end up destroying your boat.

Another important point to consider is what you can be. Of course, this depends upon you and also upon those related to you. You need a vision which inspires you to use your knowledge of yourself and others in the most appropriate way.

All of these steps must go together. You must know what you are and where you are. You must know what people around you are and where they are. And you need to know what you can be and what you want to be.

To make it easier to understand these three points, a great sage described these conditions to let us know how to be conscious about ourselves, about others, and about our future. He said that mankind is divided into three major categories:

1. Darkened sparks

2. Flickering lights

3. Radiant Suns

There are, of course, many degrees of gradation between these three.

First of all, notice that the first category is not called "dark" sparks but "darkened" sparks. **Darkened sparks** are everywhere. Once upon a time they were children of the Sun, radiant sparks projected by the Central Spiritual Sun. What happened that caused them to become darkened? Throughout ages, they used their free will consistently in the wrong direction, thus dimming their light. They did this through materialism, hatred, crime, separatism, in working against Beauty, Goodness, Justice, Joy, and Freedom.

We read in the Bible how one of two brothers became a criminal, while the other became a Blessed One. Darkened sparks, through their chain of incarnations, worked against the progress of the human race. They manipulated people, exploited them, and destroyed them. Their karma accumulated age after age and prepared the path of suffering, pain, and slavery for themselves.

It is very interesting to note that they are found in all walks of life and in all positions. Their main characteristic is that they dim the lights of others, creating separatism, exploitation, and totalitarianism. Darkened sparks will never be able to change their beingness except through the following:

a. hard work, suffering, and pain

b. striving

c. service and meditation

To increase our light, we must either suffer or strive and render service. Only through these three means can we increase our light and dispel darkness from our being.

One can strive through meditation, study, and self-confrontation. People think that they can stay as they are. Observe what happens to a fire if it is left unfed. It slowly turns to ash. The same thing happens to the spark in man. It falls into a pile of karmic ash and its light ceases to shine. But if fuel is added to the fire, the spark grows in light and radiates its beauty. We are either going to increase our light or eventually become darkened sparks.

Service is a flow of inner light through our thoughts, words, and actions. As that light increases its current, the light of our vehicles increases and gradually we become Radiant Suns.

Suppose you have a container of precious rose oil suspended above your head; service is the process of permeation of this oil into all your muscles, emotions and thoughts, and then the radiation of the oil out of your being as the most sweet fragrance through your actions.

Darkened sparks are led by their karma into places or conditions where they will be unhappy or joyless— even if they live in great luxury and have important positions. They will not be allowed to enjoy spiritual realization, expansion of consciousness, or engage in true meditation, study, and service—even if they live in temples and bury themselves in holy books.

Every time you see people suffering, people who are ignorant, people who have no understanding of spiritual values, of spiritual joy and ecstasy, remember that they desired such a condition, having planted the seeds for these conditions in the past. Do not pity them but have compassion. With your compassion you will know exactly what they can be if they plant different seeds in this life.

Flickering lights are very dangerous people. They have both light and dark moments in their lives. Through light they attract people; then through darkness, they destroy them. Flickering lights have six main characteristics.

1. They are unstable.

2. They lack firm direction and perseverance.

3. They are undependable and untrustworthy.

4. They spread confusion in the minds of others.

5. They have contradictory goals.

6. They are victims of pleasures and vanity.

1. Instability. This is a sign that a person is caught in the waves of his agitated sea of emotions, changing thought, and the ever-demanding pleasures of the body. Stability is a sign of being grounded in spiritual realities, principles, and ideas. Unstable people lead you into danger and disappointment because every moment their foundation moves—and you cannot build something permanent on a moving foundation. You cannot trust any serious duty to them or give them a responsibility upon which they can stand firm.

They are unstable in their lives as well as in their relationships. The ancients used to call them "broken boats in the hands of the waves of the sea." One day they respect you; the next day they slander you.

2. Lack of firm direction and perseverance. Flickering lights actually do not have any direction. One day they go right, the next day they go left; one day they worship, the next day they curse. They busy their minds with high ideals but visit the most obnoxious and shameful places in their daily lives.

People without firm direction are the most dangerous people. There was once a professor who claimed to be a New Age teacher. He published a few books and articles to attract people to him. Once his victims were lured, he encouraged them to use drugs, engage in prostitution, and so forth.

Some "egg-headed" ones used to say, "He is a great thinker; we must listen to his advice and use dope." Others said, "Since he is a professor, he knows what to do." This professor led many hundreds to prisons, asylums, and hospitals, but I never saw him feel sorry for what he did to these beautiful people. When he was asked why he encouraged people to use drugs, he said, "First, we live in a democracy. Second, let your children know what life is." The same flickering intellect is found in his books.

To have a direction means to go toward perfection through expansion of consciousness. If a person has no direction, his entire life will be lived as a slave to pleasure, stupidity, and greed.

3. Undependability. To depend on flickering lights is a grave mistake. They leave you at just the moment you need them the most. You cannot trust your reputation, your secrets or plans to them. In a moment of flattery or bribery, they hand you to your enemies.

The progress of humanity is carried forth only through truthful and dependable people. Every great religion or organization is founded on people who are dependable and truthful to their visions, ideals, and co-workers. No group victory is possible except with dependable and truthful co-workers. Undependable people walk with you, work with you. But when they are tempted by money, sex, and other pleasures, they suddenly disappear, leaving you alone—sometimes even in grave danger. You can find such undependable people in very high positions. They may work for a nation for twenty-five years and then turn and sell its secrets to its enemies.

Undependable people have an umbrella under which they hide. They say, "Every human being is a child of God; there is no evil in the world." Of course, these statements are traps to use people for their own interests.

You need only go to asylums, prisons, and various battlefields where human beings are destroyed daily to be convinced that there is something fundamentally wrong with humanity. To be born human is a gift of Nature; to become a real human being is the gift of human labor and striving.

It is easy to dream idealistically, but it is difficult to be a realist and see what is really going on in the world. I read of a mother who burned her child in a stove; another person killed seventeen nurses. How could the Divine Presence in them do such things? The answer is that they renounced their Divinity and became darkened sparks.

4. Confusion. The lives, literature, and speech of flickering lights are light and then dark; yes and then no. Such people gradually destroy their own and others' sense of discrimination. They become like drunk persons, falling right and left in their work.

5. Contradictory goals. With one hand they build; with the other they destroy. When they are in light, their goals are constructive; when in darkness, their goals are destructive. They try to be holy; the next day they serve evil. Today they contribute two hundred dollars to you; the next day they rob you of five hundred dollars. Today they give you a job; the next day they rob you of your purity, your dignity—or your life.

6. Pleasure and vanity. They are victims of pleasure and vanity, no matter what positions they hold or what titles they have. They can be doctors, lawyers, judges, politicians, or common people who are slaves to alcohol, sex, and money. Such people cannot lead others. If they have sensitive positions, they can easily and professionally mislead people.

To be a leader means to have stability—stability in higher ideals, honesty, and nobility.

Radiant Suns on the other hand are people who have taken at least the second or Third Initiation. The second initiation is the total purification of the heart and motives; this is fiery baptism. The Third Initiation is reached when all of the person's thoughts, emotions, expressions, actions, and deeds never again serve darkness or separatism. He never acts under hatred, fear, greed, jealousy, or revenge. He is a soul that is self-forgetful, harmless, who stands in steady light and purity.

Radiant Suns are people who have goals, plans, and purpose. They know what they are, where they are going, and how they will get there. Their intention is to be happy, healthy, prosperous, and creative. They dedicate all that they are and all that they have to the service of humanity. Their ultimate purpose is to be perfect "as their Father in heaven is perfect." They have a powerful drive toward improvement.

They are very truthful people. You can trust them with your reputation and secrets, with your plans, your jewels, money and property, your husband or wife, your children—your soul. They will not violate the will of another or his plans and will never try to alter the will, plans, or purpose of another with false excuses.

The most precious people are those you can trust. Those who are really trustworthy will one day be the treasury of a Divine Trust.

A person once asked me, "What about those who are trustworthy to the dark ones?" The answer is that forced obedience is not trust. In trust there is love, light, and freedom.

Radiant Suns are daring, courageous, and fearless. Fearful people are flickering lights or darkened sparks because they live in darkness. Courage, daring, and fearlessness are characteristics of radioactivity. Radiant Suns have the courage to stand against their own mistakes and failures. They are fearless in understanding and seeing their own stupidity. They have daring in breaking down their own limitations.

They are solemn. In contrast, there are people who are members of religious, philosophical, or even New Age groups who have read thousands of books and have attended thousands of lectures, but they still lead a shameful life that brings embarrassment to their group, friends, and relatives.

It is important to keep our dignity everywhere and live in the light of our vision. This is solemnity. Radiant Suns are embodiments of solemnity, no matter where or with whom they are.

They are firm in their devotion and dedication. They have no selfish motives; they are selfless, self-forgetful, and harmless. Their presence uplifts and enlightens people and inspires peace and serenity in others.

They live in accord with the Common Good of humanity. They have the power to penetrate into the hearts of people and lead them into the labor of world service. This sign is very profoundly explained in the Agni Yoga teaching:

> ...*The correlation of karmic conditions with the entrusting of missions can be compared to walking on a rope, but this rope has to be woven out of the most diverse materials. How much attention is needed in order to combine the threads according to color and rhythm! For, with one unrestrained exclamation one can arrest an extended work, hence I advise special caution. There exists a saying about collecting of all ropes for the journey. In an hour of tension you do not know which thread will be of use. Therefore, keep every possibility ready without reasoning whether it is small or great. For the Teacher it is always a great thing to have the definite assurance that each brief Command of His will be understood and fulfilled. Thus we advance toward the language of the heart, which is not in need of a profusion of words.*[1]

To be a Radiant Sun is the highest honor and glory of a human being. We must try to prepare for a beautiful harvest in the future by planting those seeds which will help us grow in light.

The Temple of future humanity will be built, not by darkened sparks, not by flickering lights, but by those

---

1. Agni Yoga Society, *Heart* , para. 578.

who are dedicated to the Light. It is through dedication
to Light that we transform into Light.

Chapter Thirty

The Ageless Wisdom And Service

Service, in essence, is the radioactivity of the human Core which is composed of light, love, and power.

To serve people means to release in them these supreme potentials and channel them into creative lives.

Service has its own hindrances. These are the three rattlesnakes:

- Ego

- Vanity

- Condemnation or inner judgment

These three rattlesnakes roll around you, encircle you, bite you, and put poison in you. They limit your freedom.

One of the most important characteristics of service is freedom from these three rattlesnakes. Why do they take your freedom from your hands?

Ego binds you to your lower self—and you live and act on your inferior level, identified with your self-interest. As long as you are bound to your pitiful self, you commit every kind of crime to glorify it.

Vanity binds you to the things you do not have. You are bound to something that does not exist, but these non-existing things control your life, and people feel your unreality. How can you give—serve—if you have nothing real to offer?

Condemnation binds you to the weaknesses of others, to the vices and habits of others. How can you be free if continuously your mind is identified with the weaknesses of people. How can you be free of the trash that other people have?

You cannot be a server as long as you identify yourself with the weaknesses of others because, through your condemnation, you copy their weaknesses in your character.

When a great Teacher sees that someone is identified with condemnation, He isolates that person as a society isolates a person who has a malignant and contagious disease.

Those who condemn cannot stand above the level of their condemnations, and they even fall below that level because condemnation poisons their whole psyche with various vices.

If you live close to people poisoned with the spirit of condemnation, you tie yourself to their trash can and smell it forever.

Condemnation is like injecting into your skin the vices of the others you condemn. You identify with the trash about which you talk. In condemning others you become exactly like or lower than those whom you condemn.

The great Lord said, "Judge not so that you be not judged."

When you judge or condemn others, at the same moment you already condemn yourself because you became one with those you condemned.

I have seen this. There was a pure, innocent girl, maybe twenty-one years old, who used to talk about other girls and say,

"That one is a prostitute."

"That one is laying with two persons."
"That one is pregnant."
"That one is cheating."
"That one is filthy."
"That one is dirty, but I am pure."

Years passed, and this girl became not only a prostitute but also a criminal because she occupied her consciousness continuously with the weaknesses and crimes of others.

If these three rattlesnakes exist within any person, he or she cannot be a server.

Try to avoid such people because they may poison and contaminate you. If you want to be a server, you must be extremely careful of these three rattlesnakes.

A good server is also a person who has a sword of wisdom, and he uses his sword to free people from such vipers. But, the most dangerous thing for a server is to try to make people free from these three rattlesnakes.

A server must be free from these three rattlesnakes to be able to radiate Beauty, Goodness, Righteousness, Joy, and Freedom.

Your greatest enemies often are those whom you tried to make free. Immediately when you try to free a person from his vanity, ego, and condemnation, that person attacks you with a smile or anger. The secret is that ego, vanity, and condemnation provide vehicles for dark forces, who eventually possess the person. And, if the dark ones see anyone trying to free their victims, they attack the server to prevent their victims from being freed.

This is why those who live long enough with ego, vanity, and condemnation eventually are possessed. For a long time there is no salvation for them because the possessor will not allow them to hear any advice, see any light, or taste any beauty.

People must escape from bees that attack them. Similarly, you must escape from those who spread the poisons of ego, vanity, and condemnation—if you do not have enough protection. Protection is given only if you are totally dedicated to the Most High.

There are four ways that such people of ego, vanity, and condemnation can go:

1. They burn and destroy themselves.

2. They destroy those who try to help them.

3. They repent and begin serious discipline to get rid of the possessors.

4. They give themselves to the service of humanity with a real, sacrificial spirit.

If you want to serve, you must always hold in your consciousness three principles:

- Your service will be done without expectation.

- Your heart will be filled with the joy of gratitude that an opportunity is given to you to serve.

- You will not waste time resenting those who hurt you in the past. The wheel of karma will bring them to you in the future as your servants.

The Ageless Wisdom teaches people how to serve with self-forgetfulness, harmlessness, and right speech.

Chapter Thirty-One

The New World

The goal of the Teaching is to create a new world, a world that has discovered the treasury of the heart, a world that has mastered the science of right human relations, a world that has understood the mystery of human brotherhood, a world that has seen the vision of divinity living in each human being.

A Great Teacher states that "the New World [is] the precipitation of the Invisible One."[1]

The invisible world is assumed to be the world of causes, the world of originations, the world that has less illusion.

We are challenged to strive toward "the new world," beyond our world of glamor, illusion, and constant change.

The new world is also a better image of ourselves, the image that is more real, more true, an image that is more stable, an image that is as different as the trees are different from their reflection in the lake.

It is impossible to advance unless we find a deeper reality in ourselves or a deeper world of reality beyond our daily life.

Those who have a feeling that they are somewhat better than what they appear to be are closer to the "new world."

We often have glimpses of how things could be. Such an inner glimpse of the beyond creates striving

1. Agni Yoga Society, *Heart*, para. 40.

within us to search for a better "land" in which to establish our identity.

The new world cannot be recognized unless we find something more elevated within ourselves.

Some people have a habit of shutting down their contact with the average life in the world so they can dream of a world of beauty, peace, love, joy, and freedom. This is an innate healing process, especially when things go badly and life becomes complicated. By withdrawing into such a world of beauty, people gather enough strength to face the rough world and keep their balance on the rising waves of problems.

Everyone of us has an inner sanctuary. We can go there and meet the better side of ourselves.

For some, their sanctuary is locked and they do not have access to it. For others, it is open only in severe crises. But for a few, it is always open and can be visited daily—through meditation, prayer, worship, and sacrificial service—to contact their inner resources of energy and wisdom and to enable them to continue their service, despite the many obstacles of life.

The new world is very close to us if we are daring enough to detach ourselves from the ordinary world and from our ordinary self-image.

We are told to strive into the future. It is such a striving that renews our spirit and does not let us slide down from the heights we have reached.

The future, the new world, can be traced by traveling through the higher states of consciousness and by trying to make such states of consciousness bring fruits into our life.

We cannot achieve the future unless we make the future continuously be the present.

The new world is achieved also by rejecting all those thoughts, conditions, and forms that do not agree with the ideas of inclusiveness, synthesis, and the Common Good.

Nothing can last or be new if it is separative, is based on ego and vanity, or is used to exploit and suppress others.

The new world is built by group consciousness, cooperation, and unity. These three factors demand the termination of separatism and self-interest, the termination of businesses based on exploitation and greed, and the termination of the tendency to attach to worn out traditions, customs, and habits.

The creation of a new world is imperative and unavoidable if people in the world want to end pain, suffering, unhappiness, slavery, and injustice.

The new world is within our being. One must create conditions to make it precipitate.

In the past hundred years people have stimulated human thinking and emotions by writing about utopias. This is so useful, yet most people do not realize that utopias open a path toward the new world.

People once thought that travel to the moon was a hallucination. Not everyone believed this, and now man has walked on the moon.

We can use our creative imagination to build a new world.

The dreamers of the past were vanguards for the present. The dreamers of the present will be the vanguards of the future. The Teaching stands for the future and for the actualization of the future.

Chapter Thirty-Two

Occultism Versus Black Arts

Occultism is the science of religion. Through the science of occultism one can prove that religion, in its purest form, is the application of the laws of nature and the path which leads human beings to their loftiest destiny.

People ignorantly identify occultism with "black arts." Occultism is not sorcery, black magic, mediumism, psychism, channeling, divination, hypnotism, satanism, necromancy, fortune telling, voodoo, ancestor worship, and so on and so forth.

Occultism is a royal science, a search for truth, beauty, goodness; a search for meaning, a search for purpose. Occultism is the investigation of all the laws of nature and an endeavor to use these laws to help the perfection of human nature. Occultism is the science intended to reveal the concealed Divinity in man.

Actually our space science, computer science, electronic science, space chemistry, and physics are as occult as the science of occultism is, with the difference that occultism not only deals with the laws in nature but also with the laws operating in the human mind and soul.

Inevitably science and psychology are approaching occultism. Science is dealing now with finer forces in nature, and psychology, rather parapsychology, is interested in the human soul and the potentials hidden in the human soul.

People, in order to express their hatred and to manipulate the ignorant masses, take a word and misuse it to satisfy their hatred and anger.

I remember being in a Christian monastery where a student used to hate a teacher who, in all his conversations, used to mention the name "St. ___." One day this student, while walking in the woods, saw the teacher kissing a girl.

The next day he came to the yard where students were engaged in various discussions and shouted, "St. ___ was kissing a girl." To our surprise, when we asked him what he meant, he repeated, "St. ___ was kissing a girl."

After this event, the name "St. ___" was continuously used to denote any sexual approach. Anyone in the monastery who was engaged in any kind of sexual activity was called "St. ___." Also, the teacher, who had the habit of frequently using the name of St. ___ in his conversation, was referred to as "St. ___."

In a similar way the word occultism is prostituted in some of our modern publications.

An intelligent, sincere, and solemn person will not play with words nor associate good names with ugly or destructive activities to insult those who are true occultists or the followers of a true science. This science is laboring to discover the laws of the soul and the consciousness controlling the human being, the planet, the solar system, and even the galaxy.

Occultism is the science of those who are further advanced than the present humanity. It is they who have the true knowledge of the laws of nature.

Black magic, exercised by some trained minds, is different from occultism. Black magic uses the laws of nature for selfish ends, for destruction, revenge, and hatred. But occultism uses the laws of nature to perfect oneself "as the Father in heaven is perfect."

A black magician is his own limitation, and he cannot penetrate into the laws of nature beyond a certain point. But the occultist is his own path, truth, and life.

The first one imprisons himself within the karma of his activities. The second one has the key to open all doors because he never imposes his will on others and works with the laws of nature and with the purpose of these laws.

The occultist studies the seven kinds of substance:

- physical/etheric
- astral
- mental
- Intuitional
- Atmic
- Monadic
- Divine

He studies them and the laws operating in them, and he tries to have first-hand experience of the worlds that are formed by these seven planes of substance.

He uses each law on each plane, and his experience on each plane, to further the perfection of life forms existing on those planes.

Occultism is the science not only of the **laws** of nature but also of the **energies** in nature. In a sense, our sciences are presently doing exactly what occultism was doing millions of years ago at its start: discovering the laws and the energies of nature.

Another difference between science and occultism is that science is occupied with the discovery and use of laws and energies of the physical world. Occultism is occupied with the discovery of the laws and energies of all planes of manifestation, as well as the discovery of the ultimate purpose of these energies and laws.

An occultist searches for the purpose behind these laws and energies. The laws and energies of science have been prostituted and used under the pressure of human greed, hatred, exploitation, jealousy, separatism, treason, and other self-destructive forms. One needs to see how science—with its pollutants, uncontrolled radioactivity, shock waves, misused electricity, and pesticides—has been used to lead the entire humanity to the edge of the abyss. The reason is that science has not known the purpose operating behind the laws and energies of nature—in man and in the planet.

When science discovers the true purpose of life, science will be the true occultism. It is here that the true religion can help science discover the purpose of life—gloriously formulated by Christ:

"Be perfect as your Father in heaven is perfect."

This is a formula of a supreme science to be discovered by each occultist.

It is very interesting to know that the science of today is mostly the product of physical experience and mental research. There is nothing wrong with this. But, according to the occultist, the mind and body are primitive tools which are not capable of being used to search and discover and unlock the laws and energies found on higher planes.

What would happen if a scientist operated with tools that were Intuitional, with formulas and knowledge that were Intuitional? What a vast horizon would open in front of his eyes.

Occultism says that the matter of the Intuitional Plane is as much matter as the matter of the physical plane. It goes on also to tell us that the bodies of some entities in space are built of Intuitional substance. Can you imagine what will happen when a scientist can function on the Intuitional Plane and build Intuitional devices to study the Cosmic Laws and Energies millions of light years beyond his ability to make physical contact?

Occultism is as much science as science is—with the difference that occultism works and operates in more subtle planes, with more subtle devices, and uses its knowledge of laws and energies not against nature but to cooperate with nature and bring to all beings—

East, West,

North, South,

Above, Below,

—pure bliss, harmony, freedom, and the highest spiritual achievements.

Occultism is the science of religion, but this will not be a complete definition if we do not add that it is the deeper science also of politics, education, philosophy, the arts, the sciences, and economy.

This science of occultism includes the Laws of the Seven Rays and the fields of the Seven Rays corresponding to the seven fields of human endeavor.

It is the primordial science, the knowledge that belongs to those who, with their own striving and effort, were able to discover it and pass it to those who were ready.

Another difference between any science or field of knowledge and occultism is that science welcomes any person who can learn and apply it, but occultism does not do so.

Occultism does not impart knowledge except to those who have the highest moral integrity and purity of motive and heart.

Occultism teaches that, except if the vessel is pure, occult knowledge burns and destroys it. This is why science and even religion can produce murderers from their ranks, enemies of humanity, destructive movements—but not occultism.

This is the reason why the knowledge of science can be used in good or bad ways. But occultism is used only to illuminate people, to construct the best bodies, and to lead the candidate to his Inner Glory—not only through ceremonies, knowledge, or worship but also through active sacrificial service and wisdom.

Another difference between an occultist, a religious man, and a scientist is their state of beingness. A religious man can talk and preach about immortality, heaven, and angels without having any experience with them; he will talk only through faith. A scientist can send an astronaut to the moon, but he is not able to overcome a vice or to clean from his heart a hatred or feeling of revenge. But an occultist is the embodiment of Wisdom and Beauty and Power. Without embodiment or actualization of the Wisdom he receives, and without assimilating it into his beingness, he cannot be an occultist. People who create hatred against occultism are those who never really know about it, but they have an instinctual feeling that others must be prevented from finding that treasure which may shed light on the poverty of their own beliefs.

For an occultist, Wisdom and the Teachings of Great Ones are not subjects of speculation or beliefs but actualized facts.

Once I asked a priest if he had any experience regarding the contents of his sermon. He was talking about the doors and windows of paradise, with what precious stones they were made, and how the angels were entering into and going out of the doors.

He looked into my eyes and said, "That is what is missing in me; it is all faith and belief, not facts!" He was supreme in his sincerity.

For an occultist, immortality is as much a fact as any other experience. Higher worlds are facts because he is able to visit them and increase his experiences and service. His Soul is a fact because he can converse with It.

Gradually people will see that any sincere and advanced scientist is on the path of occultism. Any genuine follower of Christ, Mohammed, Buddha, or Krishna is on the path of occultism because occultism is the search for and actualization of the highest in man and in the Cosmos.

The field of the study of occultism is as vast as Existence Itself. For example, occultism says that Space is the absolute ALL. Space has seven robes— seven veils—which are the Seven Cosmic Planes:

- Cosmic Adi (Divine)
- Cosmic Monadic
- Cosmic Atmic

- Cosmic Buddhic

- Cosmic Mental

- Cosmic Emotional

- Cosmic Physical

These seven planes are substantiations of Space in gradient degrees of Cosmic Matter. Each in turn is subdivided into seven subplanes totaling forty-nine.

The Cosmic Physical Plane is the densest and lowest plane. Its seven subplanes are formed of the

1. First Cosmic Ether .... Divine

2. Second Cosmic Ether .... Monadic

3. Third Cosmic Ether .... Atmic

4. Fourth Cosmic Ether .... Buddhic

5. Mental Plane

6. Astral Plane

7. Physical Plane; which in its turn is divided into seven sub-subplanes as follows:

   - First etheric plane

   - Second etheric plane

   - Third etheric plane

   - Fourth etheric plane

   - Gaseous plane

   - Liquid plane

   - Dense physical plane

Thus, to reach pure Space, the Mother Source, one needs to unveil the seven major veils with their forty-nine sub-veils.

The manifestation of Space is due to its inherent three characteristics:

1. Absolute duration

2. Primordial matter

3. Unconditional consciousness or absolute motion

Further, we are told that Spirit is the first differentiation of Space, and Matter—or Substance—is the first differentiation of Spirit.

It is stated in the *The Secret Doctrine* that "Spirit is matter *on the seventh plane* [the highest]; Matter is Spirit—on the lowest point of its cyclic activity; and both—are MAYA." [1]

Maya means illusion, unreality, deception. Spirit and matter are illusions. They are unreal from the viewpoint of the Absolute Space. Thus, every form in the Universe, including man, is an illusion, as far as its differentiations are concerned.

Each man in his Core is Space—absolute, unconditional Space. The Spirit of man is a differentiation of Space.

The descent of the Spark through each of the seven subplanes of the Cosmic Physical Plane creates the matter of all subplanes as its vehicles of communication. In the physical body it begins to develop its inherent consciousness. As it awakens, it builds its astral shield, then its mental shield, and feels itself as a

---

1. H.P. Blavatsky, *The Secret Doctrine*, 2 vols. (Pasadena, CA: Theosophical University Press, 1988), vol. 1, p. 633.

separate entity, a soul. Then it climbs to abstract levels of Buddhi, or the Fourth Cosmic Ether, and develops inclusive awareness. Further on it reaches the Second Cosmic Ether and develops the "I am" consciousness. This consciousness is on the Cosmic Physical Plane. Eventually the Spark graduates to the Cosmic Astral Plane where it can have the faintest vision of the journey leading to the Father's Home.

Spirit is the first differentiation of Space. Below the Spirit, on the second plane, we have Akasha.

> *Akasha. . .from which all that exists is born by separation or differentiation. It is the cause of existence; it fills all Infinite Space; is Space itself, in one sense, or both its sixth and seventh principles.*[2]

The student of occultism is the student of all these seven Cosmic Planes. He studies not only the form but also the substance, laws, energies, and forces of nature which come into being as motion passes through these forty-nine subplanes and through their various formations.

Occultism is the science of energies. It is the science of Space, Spirit, and matter in their various combinations.

It is different from the mundane science in that occultism has a supreme destiny to lead people to the Real, to their **Spacehood,** with an ever expanding consciousness, with an ever inclusive compassion and love.

Science, in general, is a servant to produce the satisfaction of physical, emotional, and mental desires, often at the expense of human welfare and the future.

---

2. *Ibid.*, vol. 2, pp. 511-512.

In occultism the lowest existence of Spirit is called the Spark, the flame, the fire in every atom and form, the life-flame in man. It is this Spark that contains in Itself the whole of Space. In the Spark exists the whole of manifestation and the Space, in which manifestation is a floating foam of bubbles.

As the Spark advances toward Space, It builds the mechanism called man, then forms Its personality— which is the collective unity of physical-etheric, emotional, and mental vehicles synthesized by the flame of the Spark. For centuries the Spark is subject to the personality. When It succeeds in emancipating Itself from the personality, we call It the human soul. And if It advances further and functions simultaneously in the higher mental body, in the Fourth Cosmic Ether (Buddhic), and in the Third Cosmic Ether (Atmic), we call the Spark, or the human soul, a *Triad* or a *Spiritual Triad*. If It further advances to the Second Cosmic Ether (Monadic), It becomes an Individuality, a Monad. If It advances one subplane more into the Divine Plane, or into the First Cosmic Ether, It is called the *Self*.

The Self is different from the Monad in that the Monad, or Individuality, sees the completion of Its age-long dream to be *Itself*, a separate, immortal power of beauty and light. But in the next degree, It begins to see the essential unity of Its Self with all other Selves on the road to the Cosmic Source.

Still, in comparison to even higher planes of achievement, the awareness of the Self is just like a primitive dream.

All this progress is achieved through a method which is called **initiation**. Initiation is expansion of consciousness and self-actualization which leads into beingness on higher and higher planes.

Science is not yet interested in immortality nor in the existence of Higher Worlds or Subtle Worlds. We can call our science one dimensional because the consciousness in operation in science does not search for other dimensions in which different levels of consciousness operate.

M.M. states:

> *Who, then, will think of success in the Subtle World, if it is not permissible to speak and think? The Teaching which does not know the Subtle World does not serve as a guide, because earthly existence is not even an hundreth part of life in the Subtle World. It means that it is useful to know the conditions of the more lasting existence.*[3]

Occultism teaches that there are forty-nine states of consciousness and, beyond them, the Absolute Consciousness.

It also teaches that every Spark in every form, from the atom to the largest galaxies, has Its own consciousness according to Its development.

Occultism does not deny the discoveries of science, nor the wisdom taught by religion, but occultism does not approve of all the uses of science, or of all its discoveries. Occultism does not approve of the pollution and the weapons created by science.

Occultism also does not agree with religious fanaticism, separatism, and exploitation. It does not agree with religious prejudices and superstitions.

---

3. Agni Yoga Society, *Heart,* para. 329.

Occultism is the pure science and the pure religion. Occultism is the future of science, once science begins to develop in harmony with the Purpose of life.

Occultism teaches also about the war in Heaven and how to bring peace not only on earth but in Heaven—in the astral and mental planes and even in the Cosmic Astral and Cosmic Lower Mental Planes.

Occultism teaches that all superhuman Beings, stars and constellations, various planets, even the Souls of planets, solar systems and galaxies, billions and billions of light years ago were human beings who conquered matter and time and advanced in their evolution toward Absolute Space.

The Higher Worlds are not a calm ocean but a stormy sea where many battles and wars rage between developing and backsliding Sparks or entities or forces of nature. We read about these wars in *The Secret Doctrine.*

> *The great "Wars in Heaven" in the Puranas; the wars of the Titans, in Hesiod and other classical writers; the "struggles," also in the Egyptian legend between Osiris and Thyphon, and even those in the Scandinavian legends, all refer to the same subject. Northern Mythology refers to it as the battle of the Flames, the sons of Muspel who fought in the field of Wigred. All these relate to Heaven and Earth, and have a double and often a triple meaning, and esoteric application to things above as to things below. They relate severally to astronomical, theogonical and human struggles; to the adjustment of orbs, and the supremacy among nations and tribes. The "Struggle of Existence" and the "sur-*

vival of the fittest" reigned supreme from the moment that Kosmos manifested into being, and could hardly escape the observant eye of ancient Sages. Hence, the incessant fights of Indra, the god of the Firmament, with the Asuras—degraded from high gods into Cosmic demons; and with Vritri or Ah-hi; the battles fought between stars and constellations, between Moon and planets—later on incarnated as kings and mortals. Hence also the War in Heaven of Michael and His Host against the Dragon (Jupiter and Lucifer-Venus), when a third of the stars of the rebellious host was hurled down into Space, and its place was found no more in Heaven. [4]

Further on in *The Secret Doctrine* it is stated:

The first war happened in the night of time, between the gods and the (A)-suras, and lasted for the period of one "divine year." On this occasion the deities were defeated by the Daityas under the leadership of Hrada. After that, owing to a device of Vishnu, to whom the conquered gods applied for help, the latter defeated the Asuras. [5]

In the *Secret Doctrine*, one war takes place before the building of the solar system; another, on Earth, at the "creation" of man; and the third "war" is mentioned as taking place at the close of the Fourth Race, between its adepts and those of the Fifth Race, that is,

---

4. *The Secret Doctrine*, vol. 1, 1988 ed., p. 202.

5. *Ibid.*, p. 419. "Divine year" is explained in the text of this source as 4,320,000,000 X 365 years.

between the Initiates of the "Sacred Island" and the sorcerers of Atlantis.

Occultism teaches that the war also goes on in each human being and in nature. The warriors are personified natural forces and energies, spirit and matter, struggling with each other to have control. But according to the legend, with the help of the "Father" the warriors who stand in harmony with the Father. . .win!

Occultism says that there was an ocean at the middle of the Gobi Desert in which there were twelve islands. Each island was in communication with one of the signs of the Zodiac. Eventually ten of them disappeared and only two islands remained on which twelve great Rishis were living. Ages later one island only remained in a small lake where, we are told, lives the Ancient of Days with His co-workers as a link between the Zodiac and the Earth.

Full moon meditation, emphasized by a great Teacher of occultism, is the time to increase the contact of the Earth with the Zodiac. This is done by special meditation at the full moon time when our Sun is in one of the zodiacal signs.[6]

The supreme duty of the followers of occultism is to bring harmony and peace and cooperation between all forces and elements of nature. Occultism believes that such a labor is a sacred labor to help the laws of nature lead the existence from its minutest and highest expressions from "Chaos to Beauty."

What relation has occultism to the Ageless Wisdom and the Teaching?

---

6. For further information on full moon mediation please refer to *Symphony of the Zodiac*, 2nd. rev. ed. by Torkom Saraydarian (Sedona, AZ: Aquarian Educational Group, 1988).

Occultism is the overall science of energies and laws, related to all planes of existence.

The Ageless Wisdom is that part of this science which has accumulated in the records of all races in various forms.

The Teaching is the appropriation of this science and the records to the needs of people, according to their capacity to assimilate and actualize.

Chapter Thirty-Three

Leadership

The image of leadership is presented to the public in a number of ways. There may be heroic images, images of greatness, and even images of degradation and failure. People who have been hurt or belittled, or who have lost an opportunity to lead, may either flatter or attack the image of a leader. The motive may vary; it may be to destroy, to gain benefit, or even to take over the leader's position in the future.

The student of Wisdom must have a pure motive when presenting the image of a leader or a man of high position or talent to the public. His motives must be to inspire people with events and words that evoke striving.

A leader's image may be subject to personality weaknesses or failures, but there is also the spiritual achievement and success that must be considered. The student of Wisdom must not occupy himself with the weaknesses and failures of the leader's image, or impress those weaknesses on the minds of the audience—except in certain cases to demonstrate how heroic it was for that leader to overcome those weaknesses to achieve great position or realization.

People are sometimes greater that their deeds. Sometimes their deeds are greater than themselves. This happens when one receives invisible help in critical conditions. Such assistance can come from the person's Soul or from a Great One interested in that person's line of work.

The student of Wisdom must find the great deeds in the life of the leader and present them to the audience to inspire them and encourage them toward worthy labor.

The Soul of the nation or the Hierarchy, foreseeing a great crisis, will send a person who can handle a crisis and open a new opportunity for the nation. Such a person can have many personality defects, but by the right of his acceptance of the labor and by the inspiration of the Higher Worlds, he does a miraculous job.

Dark forces are against such glorious achievements, and they do not want a great image of achievement to be built in the consciousness of humanity. They may unearth weaknesses of the personality and blow them out of proportion in biographies and other presentations, for example. For the dark forces, every image of heroism must be opposed, even destroyed by any possible means.

There are also idiots who want recognition, and they think the best way to get recognition is to attack a great person. Then their vanity is satisfied.

The student of Wisdom does not need to busy himself with the writings of such people. His duty is to see the beauty and present that beauty—even create beauty about the person. For example, it is written that Christ, looking at a dead dog, said, "His teeth are like pearls."

Leaders often come to the world during critical conditions, not only to render a great service but also to perfect themselves for future, more important labor. In such cases, they overcome hindrances, and with the power of their heroic sacrifice, gain victory over the personality failures and weaknesses inherited throughout the ages.

Of course, leaders must not be presented in such a glory and height that people feel discouraged and too small to reach them. But the leader must be presented as a human being who has achieved great heights and carried out his responsibilities, despite his weaknesses and because of his highly-tensed striving.

The images of great leaders are like mirrors; everyone sees himself in them. Most biographies are the biographies of the authors. Psychologically, they use the image of the leader to project themselves. One can easily see how such writers use great images secretly to present their own biographies to the world.

The student of Wisdom must study great leaders, trying to find the causes that the leader put into action to create future effects. Sometimes these effects in history are widespread and inclusive, but people try to see the leader in the limited period of his life. People cannot be evaluated righteously unless the future effects of their actions or labor are clearly seen.

Lincoln said, "Necessity knows no law." This was a very esoteric statement, and it must be understood in the proper way. Necessity emerges in a great national crisis when leaders are not able to take the time to go through legal channels to meet the crisis and bring security and opportunity.

Certain people create laws according to their level of consciousness and the need of the moment, but they do not foresee the events of the future which require new laws. People think that laws are ever-lasting; they are not. As people progress or degenerate, they evoke the construction of new laws.

Advanced leaders create new laws to meet the need. But in an emergency, they take needed action which is beyond the limits of the formulated laws. Of course, such actions may later be understood as "criminal," but true leaders risk themselves for the sake of the multitudes.

People create the following devices:

1. Laws to protect a lawmaker's interests

2. Laws to protect the lawmakers themselves

3. Laws to protect people from each other

The strongest elements in a nation, or even sometimes the majority, formulate the law. Because of our virtues or vices, some laws are temporary and some are long-lived. One thing is clear, however: Laws barely produce transformation and progress.

The greatest law is a developed sense of responsibility and conscience—based on harmlessness. To create such a law takes a long period of education and transformation. People criticize or condemn each other because of the law; and if they are clever, they create so many laws that they control the masses of people because people can no longer use these laws legally.

Imagine what a disastrous situation would result if lawmakers united to create and use laws for their own separative purposes. This is what totalitarianism is.

Great leaders, on the other hand, live for the masses and try to lead them toward unity, prosperity, health, and enlightenment. This is what we must emphasize when we speak about true leadership or even when we are presenting a legendary leader. A legendary leader who never really existed can be the vision and source of many future leaders of humanity.

In conclusion, the student of Wisdom has to promote striving toward perfection, and to do this he must present the great image in such a way that people use the image as a ladder and as a source of inspiration to transcend themselves and overcome certain limitations in their life.

Chapter Thirty-Four

How To Use The Teaching

The real Teaching must not be used for personal or group interests, for material wealth, for recognition, or for attaining positions. The primary purpose of the Teaching is to bring transformation into the lives of people.

The Teaching is given to humanity to make them shine with their innate beauty, to demonstrate goodness and righteousness, to be free and full of joy.

The Teaching is given to make people build a contact with the Higher Worlds, to bring great visions to humanity, and to unite humanity in a global brotherhood.

If people study the Teaching in order to receive diplomas, certificates, and positions, then there is the danger of using the Teaching for their personal advantage. Some people do their best to know the Teaching and to take advantage of it, but they do not use the Teaching to transform their own lives.

One must learn how to serve the Teaching, how to sacrifice for it, how to risk his life, his position, and his possessions for the Teaching. He must learn how to spread the Teaching with the spirit of self-forgetfulness.

When the Teaching is used solely to collect fortunes or to encourage people to have certificates, diplomas, and positions, the Teaching is prostituted. The Teaching must not be sold in the bazaars.

However, the Teaching needs expansions of every kind. It needs the most modern techniques, buildings, and related facilities in order to be spread. But all equipment, personnel, and buildings must be owned not as an end in itself but as the means to spread the Teaching. The purpose of the Teaching is to unfold the Divinity in man. If the equipment, labor, and buildings turn into the purpose, the spirit of the Teaching will die and only a shell will remain. Such a shell will serve as a business and will lose the power of transforming lives.

There are many groups and organizations which have lost the true purpose of the Teaching but which continue to use the Teaching to keep their organization running and the buildings in operation.

One must not make the Teaching serve himself. Instead, he must serve the Teaching. Christ said, "First search for the Kingdom of God, and all else will be given to you." People start searching for the Kingdom of God, and when "everything else is given to them," they forget the Kingdom and worship the things that are given to them. In other words, they turn into soulless organizations instead of operating as spiritual organisms.

Those who follow the Teaching will follow It with a pure heart by striving earnestly to change their life and resurrect themselves into a new life.

The Teaching will show us why and how we fail and defeat ourselves. If our purpose is to transform our life, we must keep the light of the Teaching always present in our consciousness, and walk on our daily path to spread the light of the Teaching.

Once we exploit the Teaching, the Teaching leaves us. When this happens, we fall into a life of pretension, imitation, hypocrisy, materialism, vanity, and ego.

The Teaching must be spread through the actualization of the wisdom that we discover in it. The Teaching must be spread through the power of the transformation of our life.

The Teaching must be spread because of its power to bring vitality into the lives of people.

The Teaching must be spread through demonstrating it in our life through

1. detachment and non-identification

2. renunciation

3. sacrificial service

4. compassion

5. forgiveness

6. gratitude

7. solemnity

8. nobility

The followers of the Teaching must serve humanity as the embodiment, as the living examples of the Teaching.

Those who have personal interests in the Teaching will slowly be cast out by the power of the Teaching.

The signs that they are being cast out are these:

1. They no longer enjoy reading about the Teaching.

2. They no longer understand it.

3. The Teaching becomes repulsive. They search for faults in those who are in the Teaching. They criticize and slander them.

Life creates problems for them and draws them away from the Teaching. But life never forgets them. Years and lives later, it brings them there where they left the Teaching and makes them serve the Teaching with the same intensity that they slandered the Teaching in the past.

The Teaching never punishes people but offers all the needed elements that make people happy, healthy, successful, and cooperative.

After a person is enlightened by the Teaching, he offers his life for the Teaching. And nothing can slow down his progress in life toward higher spiritual realizations.

Chapter Thirty-Five

Fiery Path And The Teaching

Fire can aggravate all illness, therefore great attention should be paid to the state of fiery striving.[1]

What is fiery striving?

Fiery striving is

1. Conscious effort to surpass our beingness

2. Persistent effort to reach the ideal state of consciousness to which we aspire

3. Total dedication to the Common Good

4. Devotion to the highest principles and ideas

5. Fervent meditation

6. Steady effort to control our physical activities, emotional reactions, and our thoughts

7. Firm longing to come in contact with higher realities

8. Labor to stand in the light of the Spiritual Triad or to constantly be fused with pure light, love, and energy

---

1. Agni Yoga Society, *Fiery World*, 3 vols. (New York: Agni Yoga Society, 1969), vol. I, para. 53.

These are fiery strivings and people who commit themselves to such efforts must know that the fiery energy increases in them and that this "fire can aggravate all illnesses."

All disorders and unhealthy conditions of the bodies come to the surface, causing great distress, discomfort, and problems in the lives of those "who dare for a fiery striving." This is why the leaders of fiery strivings are prepared from their childhood to be ready to carry on fiery duties and responsibilities. Life creates all possibilities to purify their nature and make their mental, astral, and physical mechanisms ready to carry the fire without being burned by it. The Teachers advise us to abide in mental purity, emotional purity, and physical purity because, as we engage ourselves more and more with fiery striving, the spots of impurities become inflamed, causing mental, astral, and physical damage.

Spiritual striving puts a great pressure on all our vehicles, and hidden weaknesses come to the surface. This is why the Teaching advises us to be extremely cautious and follow the guidance of our Teachers to establish ourselves firmly on the fiery path.

We are told that a long period of preparation is needed to eradicate from our nature all physical, emotional, and mental impurities, such as habits, uncontrolled urges and drives, vices, hatred, fear, anger, jealousy, revenge, malice, gossip, slander, and treason in the physical and emotional realms, and in the mental realms, vanity, egotism, separatism, greed, lies, hypnotic suggestions, self-interest, indifference toward the pains and sufferings of others, irresponsibility, and their like.

These are illnesses that can be aggravated under the fire of striving and gradually affect our physical body with other illnesses and diseases. This state causes distressing conditions in our family, group, environment, and in all our relationships.

Those who lose their path develop "forbiddance." They involve themselves in controlling people's relationships. They become unpleasant, dour, grim, threatening, offensive. They lose their spirit of forbearance and sink into the pit of irritation. Such a state of consciousness does not work in their favor, and gradually they lose their reasoning and logic in a thick mist of self-righteousness.

It is observed that those who prematurely expose themselves to the Teaching—in the form of religion and philosophy or in the form of arts and creativity or meditation and spiritual discipline—pass through a hard time if impurities exist in them. Some of them go berserk or demonstrate mental imbalance. They yield to the forces of hatred and destruction. Physically they experience various pains and illnesses and involve themselves in treason and slander and end their life in misery or even suicide.

Whenever a person decides to walk the fiery path, he must listen to his Teacher who will warn him and guide his steps until the fires of his nature are harmonized and his psychic energy is in control.

Those who start the Path and then abandon it, following their impurities, become problems in their environment. They captivate people with their bright side, then poison them with their dark side until people start realizing the situation. On the other hand, when a person has a considerable amount of true love, selflessness, and purity in his nature, he flourishes and blooms as he enters the Path. His latent talents, his sleeping potentials, the innermost beauty he has, all begin to manifest, spreading health, happiness, prosperity, light, magnetism, and guidance throughout his environment.

Many sicknesses or diseases disappear because of the increase of fire. New opportunities reveal themselves, co-workers are attracted, and every kind of help is given to those who really follow the Path.

Most of our mental, emotional, and physical problems are caused by a lack of nourishment. The Teaching is the best nourishment which cures, heals, and regenerates all our systems and helps us penetrate into higher levels of consciousness and beingness.

Real Teachers watch closely the students of fiery striving and follow them in compassion and forgiveness because the first target of sick people are their Teachers. Their Teachers, for a long period of time, become absorbers of their poisons, become their trash can. But the Teachers forgive them because they realize that in the past they themselves did similar things to their own Teachers. Those students who, with humility, persistence, and gratitude, follow the guidance of their Teacher eventually pass through the dark tunnel and emerge into daylight. They are surprised and wonder what a great and sacrificial help was given to them by their Teachers to lead them to light.

In old stories, before a knight began his journey, his mother would give him three jewels. They were the symbols of humility, persistence, and the spirit of gratitude. It is only by carrying these three jewels on the Path that a disciple completes his purification process and eventually joins those who are involved in fiery service for the Hierarchy.

We are often asked if those who lose their Path and damage their mechanisms can have hope, in their moments of consciousness, to return to the Path and complete their training?

The answer is yes. *Life is, in itself, an opportunity and we have an opportunity every moment to return to the Path,* but the farther we go away from the Path, the more effort must be made to return to it; therefore, the sooner we return to the Path, the less damage we do to ourselves and to others. Hence we build less karma.

Some ignoramuses, when they read these pages will wonder if by the Path we mean any specific group, organization, religion, or ideology?

The Path can be defined clearly as a steady effort to serve Beauty, Goodness, Righteousness, Joy, and Freedom, and live in gratitude and harmlessness to bring health, happiness, prosperity, and enlightenment to all people everywhere.

Groups, organizations, and ideologies can be considered centers through which focused service is rendered, but they are not the Path, especially when crystallizations and personality problems damage the free flow of love, respect, and humility.

The Teaching must be assimilated within our hearts and put into practice in our daily life in all our mental, emotional, and physical relationships. The main goal of the Teaching is to purify our nature, to increase our psychic energy, to equip us with the fire of dedication, to cultivate in us an intuitional discrimination, and to enable us to offer all that we are for the service of One Humanity.

Chapter Thirty-Six

Evolving Wisdom

Does the Ageless Wisdom evolve or progress? The answer is yes. The Ageless Wisdom evolves and progresses as new and more advanced Initiates bring their treasures of experience and beingness from objective and subjective worlds. Also, the Ageless wisdom evolves and progresses as new and more advanced disciples begin reinterpreting it according to their achievement.

It is the needs of people, their aspiration, striving, and spiritual expectations that, as a mighty current of invocation, cause the Wisdom to manifest in greater fullness.

The Ageless Wisdom is an ocean into which mighty rivers of Light are pouring at every moment—to be understood, conquered, and used. It is an ever regenerating ocean which supports human life and prepares humanity to face Space, which is the Source of all Wisdom.

The Ageless Wisdom is the ocean of Light, Love, and Power, and every Great One is a wave, rhythmically washing on the shores of human consciousness. But we must remember that the ocean of Light which we call the Ageless Wisdom already exists in Space, with many layers of magnitude. Great, Great Beings, Lives, and Buddhas—throughout billions of years— spoke about this Wisdom in its three main divisions:

— Who are we.

— What is the Purpose of all manifestation.

— How can we actualize this Purpose.

Some people are directly and entirely involved with these three *diamonds.* Others are occupied with the pebbles of the sea. Others are living as automatons. But the exciting point is that *Wisdom exists,* and it is the science by which all is manifested. It is our duty to learn this science and do our "whole duty in our journey to His sacred feet."

The Ageless Wisdom that exists in Space is distributed by Great Ones in all worlds. Each world has its own quota, according to its capacity to receive, assimilate, and actualize the amount of Wisdom given to it. Every world can receive more from Space, if the living beings of that world assimilate that which has already been given to them. This is why Christ said, "To those who have more, more will be given." To "have" means to have the capacity to assimilate.

As in the Universe, so also within our inner, small world. Our Self sets the limit for our Wisdom. The more we live and actualize the Wisdom, the more we receive; and the more we give, the more we receive.

The Ageless Wisdom evolves not only within each human soul, through his striving and actualization, but also in the entire Space, in the entire Universe. Thus, contrary to human superstition, the Source of creation also *evolves,* and with each step of Its evolution, the greater magnitudes of Its glory are revealed.

Ten Greater Powers In Man

1. The power that enables you to be indifferent toward all praise, flattery and appreciation of yourself.

2. The power that makes you not to be defeated by your past mistakes, not to react to your slanderers, and not to feel defeated by them.

3. The power that keeps you in tune with the directions of the Cosmic Magnet.

4. The power that impels you to continue fufilling your duties and responsibilities in spite of adverse conditions.

5. The power that enables you to stay indifferent when crows ornament themselves with your discarded feathers.

6. The power to love those who enjoy damaging your reputation.

7. The power that enables you to defend those who are under attack.

8. The power to walk away from all who are emotionally attached to you.

9. The power to continue your spiritual striving even when those around you give up.

10. The power not to hurt people and to remain harmless in your thoughts, words, and actions.

ABOUT THE AUTHOR

This is Torkom Saraydarian's latest published book. Many more will be released very soon. His vocal and instrumental compositions number in the hundreds and are being released.

The author's books have been used all over the world as sources of guidance and inspiration for true New Age living based on the teachings of the Ageless Wisdom. Some of the books have been translated into other languages, including German, Dutch, Danish, Portuguese, French, Spanish, Italian, Greek, Yugoslavian, and Swedish. He holds lectures and seminars in the United States as well as in other parts of the world.

Torkom Saraydarian's entire life has been a zealous effort to help people live healthy, joyous, and successful lives. He has spread this message of love and true vision tirelessly throughout his life.

From early boyhood the author learned first-hand from teachers of the Ageless Wisdom. He has studied widely in world religions and philosophies. He is in addition an accomplished pianist, violinist, and cellist and plays many other instruments as well. His books, lectures, seminars, and music are inspiring and offer a true insight into the beauty of the Ageless Wisdom.

Torkom Saraydarian's books and music speak to the hearts and minds of a humanity eager for positive change. His books, covering a large spectrum of human existence, are written in straightforward, unpretentious, clear, and often humorous fashion. His works draw on personal experiences, varied and rich. He offers insight and explanations to anyone interested in applying spiritual guidelines to everyday life. His no-nonsense approach is practical, simple, and readily accessible to anyone who is interested in finding real meaning in life.

Torkom Saraydarian has de-mystified the mysteries of the Ageless Wisdom. He has made the much needed link between the spiritual and the everyday worlds.

Look for exciting new books and music being released by Torkom Saraydarian.

GLOSSARY

Antahkarana: The path, or bridge, between the higher and lower mind, serving as a medium of communication between the two. It is built by the aspirant himself. It is threefold: the consciousness thread, anchored in the brain; the life thread, anchored in the heart; and the creative thread anchored in the throat. More commonly called the Rainbow Bridge.

Arhats: Ancient term designating Fourth Degree Initiates.

Ashram: Sanskrit word, refers to the gathering of disciples and aspirants which the Master collects for instruction. There are seven major Ashrams, each corresponding to one of the Rays, each forming groups or foci of energy.

Astral body: The vehicle composed of astral substance, that in which the emotional aspect of humanity expresses itself. Also known as the subtle body.

Astral Plane: The sixth plane of the Cosmic Physical Plane, in which the emotional processes are carried on. Sometimes called the astral or emotional world. Also known as the Subtle World or the Astral Realm.

Atlantis: (Atlantean Epoch). The continent that was submerged in the Atlantic ocean, according to the occult teaching and Plato. Atlantis was the home of the Fourth Root Race, whom we now call the Atlanteans.

Aura: The sum-total of all emanations from all the vehicles of any living thing.

Chakra: Energy vortex found in each vehicle, relating to a particular part of the human body. There are seven primary chakras starting from the top of the head: (1) crown, (2) brow, (3) throat, (4) heart, (5) navel, (6) generative organs, (7) base of spine.

Chalice: See Lotus.

Chohan: A person who has accomplished the Sixth Initiation.

Core: The essence or spark of God within each being; the Monad.

Cosmic Heart: See Cosmic Magnet.

Cosmic Magnet: The invisible center of the Universe.

Cosmic Physical Plane: Refers to the totality of the seven subplanes of manifestation, from highest to lowest: Divine, Monadic, Atmic, Intuitive or Buddhic, Mental, Emotional or Astral, and Physical. Each with seven subdivisions, totaling 49 planes of manifestation. (See Chapter 3).

Cosmic Self: That great Entity which pervades and sustains all things on all levels of existence.

Dark Forces: Conscious agents of evil or materialism operating through the elements of disunity, hate, and separativeness.

Disciple: A person who tries to discipline and master his threefold personality, and manifests efficiency in the field where he works and serves.

Divine Plan: See Plan.

Divine Self: See Monad.

Ego: The human soul identified with the lower vehicles (physical, emotional, and mental) and their false values.

Etheric Body: The counterpart of the dense physical body, pervading and sustaining it. Formed by matter of the four etheric subplanes. The blueprint on which the physical body is based.

Great Ones: Beings who have taken the Fifth Initiation or beyond.

Guardian Angel: See Solar Angel.

Hierarchy: The spiritual Hierarchy, whose members have triumphed over matter and have complete control of the personality, or lower self. Its members are known as Masters of Wisdom Who are custodians of the Plan for humanity and all kingdoms evolving within the sphere of Earth. It is the Hierarchy that translates the Purpose of the Planetary Logos into a Plan for all kingdoms of the planet.

Higher Centers: Refers to the crown, brow, throat, and heart centers or chakras, as well as to the centers in the higher bodies.

Higher Realms: See Higher Worlds.

Higher Self: Refers to the Solar Angel or Transpersonal Self. See also Self.

Higher Spheres: See Higher Worlds.

Higher Worlds: Those planes of existence that are of a finer vibration of matter than the physical plane. Generally refers to the higher mental plane and above.

Human soul: See soul.

Initiate: A person who has taken an initiation. See also Initiation.

Inner Core: See Core.

Inner Guide: See Soul.

Inner Presence: The Solar Angel. See Soul.

Initiation: The result of the steady progress of a person toward his life's goals, achieved through service and sacrifice, and manifested as an expansion of one's consciousness. It represents a point of achievement marked by a level of enlightenment and awareness. There are a total of nine Initiations that the developing human soul must experience in order to reach the Cosmic Heart.

Karma, Law of: The Law of Cause and Effect or attraction and repulsion. "As you sow, so shall you reap."

Lemurian Epoch: A modern term first used by some naturalists and now adopted by Theosophists to indicate an era dealing with the period of the continent Lemuria, which preceded Atlantis. The Third Root Race.

Logos, Solar: The Core of the whole Solar System and all that exists in the Solar System. His purpose is to integrate, correlate and synchronize all Centers using His Light, Love, Power—like an electrical energy—to circulate within each atom on through all Centers, thus revealing the Purpose for existence and challenging all forms to strive toward the highest form of cooperation.

Logos, Planetary: The Soul of the planet. The planet is His dense physical body to provide nourishment for all living forms.

Lotus: Also known as the Chalice. Found in the second and third mental plane (from the top.) Formed by twelve different petals of energy: three love petals, three knowledge petals, three sacrifice petals. The innermost three petals remain folded for ages. They are the dynamic sources of these outer petals. The Lotus contains the essence of all of a person's achievements, true knowledge, and service. It is the dwelling place of the Solar Angel.

Lower Psychism: The ability to perceive subtle aspects of existence with the aid of the lower centers in the human body. Mediums, channels, etc. are considered lower psychics.

Lower self: The personality vehicles of the human soul. See also the self.

Masters: Individuals Who had the privilege to master their physical, emotional, mental, and Intuitional bodies.

Meditation: Technique to penetrate the mind of the planet and develop creative abilities to manifest that mind in the life of humanity. (For in-depth information, please refer to *The Science of Meditation* and *Psyche and Psychism* by Torkom Saraydarian.)

Mediumistic: A tendency of certain individuals to astral phenomena and its perception thereof. Mediumistic people can, without guidance, fall into various dangers and traps associated with the astral plane. (For more information, see *Psyche and Psychism* by Torkom Saraydarian.)

Mental Body: The vehicle composed of the substance of the mental plane in which humanity expresses itself through thought.

Maya: A counterpart of illusions and glamors on the etheric plane. It results in the inability of the physical, emotional, and mental bodies to respond clearly to incoming impressions.

Mental Plane: There are seven planes through which a human being travels and which make up human consciousness. From the lowest level upward, they are called: Physical, Emotional or Astral, Mental, Intuitional or Buddhic, Atmic, Monadic, Divine. The Mental Plane itself is divided into seven levels. The first three from the bottom are numbers seven, six, and five, which form the Lower Mental Plane. Number four is the middle mind or link. Numbers three, two, and one form the Higher Mental Plane.

Mental Realms: See Mental Plane. Also known as the Fiery World.

Mind, Higher and Lower: See Mental Plane.

Monad: See Self.

Nirvana: The plane of consciousness known as the Atmic Plane.

One Self: The universal Life Soul pervading all existence.

Personality: Totality of physical, emotional, and mental bodies of man.

Petals: See Lotus.

Plan: The formulation of the Purpose of the Planetary Logos into a workable program—a plan—by the Planetary Hierarchy for all kingdoms of nature.

Purpose: That which the Solar Logos is intended to achieve at the end of the evolution of the Solar System. The Plan is the formulation of this Purpose for our planet only.

Race: The Ageless Wisdom divides human development into seven sections, called Root Races. From ancient times to the present, they have been called: Polarian Race, Hyperborean Race, Lemurian Race, Atlantean Race, Aryan Race, Sixth Root Race, Seventh Root Race. The latter two are the future states of human development. (For more information, see *Psyche and Psychism* by Torkom Saraydarian.)

self: The small "s" self is the sumtotal of the physical, emotional, and mental bodies of man. Commonly called the "lower self" or personality.

Self: The capital "S" Self is another term used to refer to the Core of the human being. The true Self is the developing, unfolding human soul who is trying to liberate himself, go back to his Father, and become his true Self.

Seven Fields of Human Endeavor: The expression of the Seven Rays in human evolution, each corresponding to a specific Ray. They are: Politics, Education and Psychology, Philosophy, Arts, Science, Religion, Economics and Finance.

Seven Rays: These are the seven primary Rays through which everything exists. They are pure energy, vibrating to a specific frequency and condensing from plane to plane, from manifestation to manifestation. The three primary Rays or Rays of Aspect are: The First Ray of Power, Will and Purpose; The Second Ray of Love-Wisdom; The Third Ray of Active, Creative Intelligence. There are four Rays of Attribute: The Fourth Ray of Harmony through Conflict; The Fifth Ray of Concrete Science or Knowledge; The Sixth Ray of Idealism or Devotion; The Seventh Ray of Synthesis or Ceremonial Order. These Rays indicate qualities that pertain to the seven fields of human endeavor or expression.

Solar Angels: Very advanced beings who sacrificed their life, descending from Higher Worlds to help the evolution of humanity, and guide its steps toward initiation. This happened on our planet at the middle of the Lemurian period. They are also called Guardian Angels, or Flames.

soul: With small "s" is the human psyche, the Spark, traveling on the path of evolution having three powers: willpower, attraction, and intelligence to guide its development. Also known as the evolving human soul.

Soul: Also known as the Solar Angel.

Soul Awareness: The human soul's awareness of the Solar Angel or the awareness of the human soul in the Intuitional Plane.

Spark: Human Monad fallen into matter.

Spiritual Triad: The field of awareness of the human soul. This field comes into being when the magnetic fields of the Mental permanent atom, the Buddhic permanent atom, and the Atmic permanent atom fuse and blend.

Subtle World: Refers to the astral or emotional plane.

Three-fold personality: The three vehicles of man. The combined forces and vehicles in which the evolving human soul expresses himself and gains experience during incarnation. These vehicles are the physical body, the emotional or astral body, and the mental body.

Transpersonal Self: The Solar Angel, the Inner Guide.

Treasure House: Symbolic term for the Chalice. Also called the Treasury.

Upanishads: Mystical treatises forming the *Veda*, said to date approximately from the Sixth Century, B.C. *The Upanishads* are said to be the source of all six systems of Hindu philosophy.

Vedas: Consists of four collections of writings. The *Rig-Veda*, the *Sama-Veda*, the *Yajur-Veda*, and the *Athar-Vaveda*. *The Vedas* are the Divine Revelation of the scriptures of the Hindus, from the root *viv*, "to know," or "divine knowledge."

Index

A

Absolute Consciousness - 282
Absolute devotion - 279
Absolute Space - 279
Absoluteness
   in Teaching - 105
Acceptance
   of others - 53
Accidents - 198
Accuracy - 192
Achievement - 203
Actions - 232
Activities
   mental - 177
Actualization - 304
   of brotherhood - 237
   of potentials - 132
   of the Teaching - 55
Advancement - 40, - 99
Advancement of humanity - 17
Advice - 266
Africa - 79
The Ageless Wisdom - 15, - 22, - 36,
   - 228, -266, - 285, - 303
   access to - 19
   actualization of - 42
   aim of students - 181
   an accumulation - 20
   and advancement - 109
   and beingness - 37
   and certainty - 73
   and consciousness - 37, - 40, - 73
   and discrimination - 31
   and distortion - 113
   and experience - 197
   and fanatics - 82
   and Great Ones - 85
   and holism - 266
   and life - 73
   and meditation - 30, - 211
   and myths - 20
   and occultism - 285
   and preparedness - 181
   and principles - 24 - 25
   and purpose - 73
   and readiness - 182
   and service - 31
   and Teachers - 79

and the future - 85
and the human soul - 55
and the Path - 43
and the Plan - 73
and three bodies - 181
and usefulness - 182
and Wholeness - 236
application of - 55, - 177
as a jewel - 83
as a network - 16
as a path - 24
as a science - 304
as an inspiration - 24
as an ocean - 303
as foundation - 52
as heritage - 21
as Light - 179
assimilation of - 33, - 41, - 211
characterization of - 179
converting others - 74
dangers of - 55
defined - 19, - 25, - 123
diamonds of - 304
differences in - 27
distribution of - 304
Divine intent - 23
encouragement of - 33
essence of - 27
evolution of - 303
existence of - 303
formulation of - 52
fundamentals of - 29
giver of - 81
goal of - 179
greater manifestation of - 303
guidelines to living - 24
how given - 124
how to read - 34 - 35
how to study - 34
imparting of - 81 - 82
in 20th century - 80
in seven fields - 41
in space - 303
major divisions of - 304
major goal of - 43
manifestations of - 27
parts of - 25, - 81
places of Teaching - 79
planning for - 34
practice of - 41
principles of - 27
progression of - 303

B

M

Bibliographic References

Agni Yoga Society. New York: Agni Yoga Society.
>   *Aum* , 1959.
>   *Brotherhood*, 1962.
>   *Fiery World,* Vol. I., 1969
>   *Heart*, 1934.
>   *Hierarchy,* 1944, 1977.
>   *Supermundane*, Unpublished Writings.

Balyoz, Harold. Flagstaff, AZ: Altai Publishers.
>   *Three Remarkable Women*, 1986.

Blavatsky, H. P. Pasadena, CA: Theosophical University Press.
>   *The Secret Doctrine*. 2 vols., 1988.

Blavatsky, H. P. London, Theosophical Publishing Society.
>   *The Secret Doctrine*. 3rd. rev. ed., 3 vols. 1893.

Lamsa, George M., trans. Nashville, TN: Holman Bible Publishers.
>   *The New Testament,* 1968.

Saraydarian, Torkom. Agoura, CA: Aquarian Educational Group.
>   *The Bhagavad Gita,* trans., 1974.
>   *Christ, the Avatar of Sacrificial Love,* 1974.
>   *Five Great Mantrams for the New Age,* 1975.
>   *The Psyche and Psychism,* 1981.
>   *The Science of Meditation*, 1981
>   *The Spring of Prosperity,* 1982.

Saraydarian, Torkom. Sedona, AZ: Aquarian Educational Group.
>   *Challenge For Discipleship*, 1986.
>   *Symphony of the Zodiac,* 2nd rev. ed., 1988.
>   *Triangles of Fire,* 2nd. rev., 1988.

Saraydarian, Torkom. West Hills, CA: T.S.G. Enterprises
>   *A Commentary on Psychic Energy*, 1989.

Upanishads
>   *Brihad Aranyaka Upanishad*
>   *Taittiriya Upanishad*

Other Works by **Torkom Saraydarian**

Bhagavad Gita
Challenge For Discipleship
Christ, The Avatar of Sacrificial Love
A Commentary on Psychic Energy
Cosmic Shocks
Cosmos in Man
A Daily Discipline of Worship
Dialogue With Christ
Fiery Carriage and Drugs
Five Great Mantrams of the New Age
Flame of Beauty, Culture, Love, Joy
Hiawatha and the Great Peace
Hidden Glory of the Inner Man
Hierarchy and the Plan
Irritation—The Destructive Fire
I Was
Joy and Healing
Legend of Shamballa
The Psyche and Psychism
The Psychology of Cooperation and Group Consciousness
Questioning Traveler and Karma
Science of Becoming Oneself
Science of Meditation
The Sense of Responsibility in Society
Sex, Family and the Woman in Society
Spring of Prosperity
Symphony of the Zodiac
Synthesis
Talks on Agni
Torchbearers
Triangles of Fire
Unusual Court
Woman, Torch of the Future

Next Release: **Other Worlds**

Write to the publisher for additional information regarding:

- Free catalog of author's books and music tapes.

- Information regarding lecture tapes and videos.

- Placement on mailing list.

- Information on new releases.

- Additional copies of *The Ageless Wisdom:*

U.S. $16.00, $2.00 Postage within U.S.A.
Plus applicable state sales tax.

Visions for the 21st Century®
P.O. Box 7068
Cave Creek, AZ 85331-7068 U.S.A.
Tel: (602) 502-1909
Fax: (602) 502-0713